# P.S. I Love Lucy

# Lucille Ball's
# Palm Springs

## Connect with the Author

Twitter.com/EricGMeeks
Facebook.com/Eric.G.Meeks
Eric@PSCelebrityHomes.com

## The Works of Eric G. Meeks

### Fiction
The Author Murders
Witch of Tahquitz
Six Stories

### Non-Fiction
P.S. I Love Lucy: Lucile Ball's Palm Springs
The Best Guide Ever to Palm Springs Celebrity Homes
Lawrence Welk's First TV Champagne Lady: Roberta Linn
Intuitive Reflections: The Art of Ron Klotchman
Not Now Lord, I've Got Too Much to Do
A Brief History of Copyright Law
Reversing Discrimination

### Edited by Eric G. Meeks
1853 Cavalry Quest for a Southwest Railroad Route

# P.S. I Love Lucy

# Lucille Ball's Palm Springs

# ERIC G. MEEKS

Horatio Limburger Oglethorpe, Publisher

P.S. I Love Lucy
Lucille Ball's Palm Springs
© November 2014


ISBN-13: 978-0-9862189-3-4
ISBN-10: 0-9862189-3-6

Hardback Edition


Updated 2-22-2016


Horatio Limburger Oglethorpe, Publisher

The cover photo and photo the opposite title page are of
Lucille Ball lounging in one of the large bay windows
at the El Mirador hotel during the late 1930s.
Courtesy of the Palm Springs Historical Society.

Printed in the United States of America

For my daughters
Anastasia, Alexandra, Zhanna and Gabrielle


A special thank you to
Kathy Baskerville
for her help in editing this book
and to
the Palm Springs Historical Society,
the Palm Springs Villager,
Paul Pospesil, Gail Thompson, and
Tracy Conrad for their contribution of
vintage Lucy and Desi photographs.

# Table of Contents

*Foreword*

FACTS AND LEGENDS. Research and innuendo.

Finally, I'd had enough. They were right.

In my first edition of this book, I took liberties with P.S. I Love Lucy: The Story of Lucille Ball in Palm Springs (notice: The Story of). I had some great photos, but not a lot of facts. My book sold. Some loved the book. Some fans of Lucille Ball saw the shallowness of the tale. They responded with negative reviews on Amazon. And, rightly so.

I wanted to improve the tale. The best parts of my book were the pictures. But it needed more. So – and, this may sound weird – I determined to learn as much about Lucy as I could and I read my first real biography about her, Love Lucy, the one self-written by Lucy herself and published by her daughter Lucie Arnaz. In it I found a real person – two actually: mother and daughter – not just the Lucille Ball known as a comedienne of TV legends; a flesh and blood, emotional, love-stricken small-town girl done well with feelings and desires and foibles and successes… and kids.

You see it was Lucy's daughter, Lucie, who struck me hardest. It was when in her foreword, she talked about her mom and dad and the people who she had to be wary of: reporters, money-grabbers, shysters. These selfish individuals all wanted to take a portion of her mother's memories and profit from them, with a callous disregard for who Lucille Ball really was. Stripping her dignity. Twisting the truth to satisfy their own pocketbook. Letting greed an tabloid yellow journalistic piracy rule the memory of the woman who was Lucie Jr.'s #1 person in her life. Her mom. When considering the first rendition of my P.S. I Love Lucy story I realized I had myself become a shyster.

So, the answer was simple, I determined not to be one.

In her forward, Lucie Arnaz discussed Lucille Ball's and Desi Arnaz's deaths and how Lucie and Desi, Jr. coped with funeral planning and taking over their mother's estate. (Desi Sr. had died three years prior). Every item a personal memento. Every item a collector's piece. More than ever the two adult children wanted their mother all to themselves. I felt very small for the liberties I had taken with my story; Lucille Ball, her children, her fans, they all deserved better.

With her fans openly and angrily critiquing the first edition of P.S. I Love Lucy and Lucie Arnazes words of solemn tears about the respect her mother deserved ringing in my ears, I decided to learn more about this lady who I had photographic proof of a history in Palm Springs. I would use not only the Palm Springs library resources – which is vast – but, I was determined to read as much as possible and glean from those who had written before.

I found that in many books about Lucille Ball, there were often paragraphs written about her forays into the desert. But still, I knew there had to be more. Somewhere, there was a book. I took notes. Gathered leads. Searched for clues. Researched more, and wrote the chapters you see before you, until it was a true book worthy of Lucille Ball's name.

She and Desi both had histories here. They frequented here. They romanced here. They dreamed here in Palm Springs. They built and rebuilt their lives here.

Lucille Ball and Desi Arnaz escaped to Palm Springs originally for a private interlude, an escape from their very public lives, to give their love for each other a chance to grow. Then they grew in love with the very place in which they'd first sought refuge. Many people do this. Palm Springs has an allure, a magnetic fondness which draws many people back again and again, a beauty. It is the oasis that captivates. Some, once stricken with the love of the desert never leave.

I hope in this expanded rendition of their tale I deliver the sort of facts Lucy and her fans deserve. If I've learned one thing while writing this book, it's this: Lucy deserves the best. She was a hard working, real life woman who made her life her way. Her fans love her because they know this. Her TV persona made her famous, but her fans love her not just for the roles she played; they love her for how she played at life, for the ups and downs of her successes and failures in life, in business and in love.

Lucy deserves better and so do her fans.

I hope this book is the chapter of her life that her fans never got to read before. I hope I've done the Queen of Comedy justice with what I've written here. I hope her and Desi's daughter, Lucie, and their son Desi Jr. don't think me a shyster just wanting to make a buck off their parents name and that their fans don't think me a ne'er do well who just wants to make up stories about their past in Palm Springs.

I've tried. I've really tried hard to tell the truth, the whole truth and nothing but the truth, this time around. There may be times I have to speculate because research only takes you so far. But I'll keep to the facts as far as I can and if I utilize the innuendo of speculation, I'll state it openly and let you draw the ultimate conclusion.

In the pages that follow, you will read the facts about Lucy and Desi and their histories in Palm Springs. Some will be flattering. Some will not. I am just the storyteller. But here are the truths as I've learned them.

# 1911-1933
## A Short Bio of Lucy

LUCILLE DESIREE BALL: Born August 6, 1911 in Jamestown, New York, the daughter of Henry Durrell Ball and Desiree "Dede" Evelyn Hunt. Lucy had one younger sibling, Frederick Henry Ball, born July 17, 1915. Her father died when she was only four and she was then shuffled around Northern New York as her mother looked for work. DeDe remarried four years later. Lucy was then placed with her new father's parents: a stuffy old Swedish couple. Her new grandfather was a Shriner and when his club needed entertainers she was made to audition for the chorus line. She was twelve. Lucy loved the praise she received and the entertainer in her woke up for the first time.

At 14, Lucy was sent to the John Murray Anderson School for the Dramatic Arts in New York City, more as a way to break up her young romance with a 23 year old local hood than anything else. While there, she met another future starlet, Bette Davis, though the two did not have a significant friendship.

By the age of 17, while most American ladies her age were dancing the Charleston, drinking at speak easies and wearing scandalously shortened above the knee pencil dresses with short bob-like hair styles, Lucy had landed a job as a fashion model for Hattie Carnegie, who owned retail clothing stores and was a prominent designer of high-end women's clothing. Unfortunately, Lucy became ill with Rheumatic Fever and had to move back to Jamestown for two years. She moved again to New York in 1932 and resumed her career as an actress and model. This time, she most often portrayed the perennial blonde bride and was the anchor of Carnegies fashion shows.

Besides modeling, she landed the position as the poster girl for Chesterfield Cigarettes, and while using the name Diane Belmont, began work as a chorus girl on Broadway. But, these jobs didn't last and often she was fired as fast as she was hired.

Still, Lucy struggled, and she would sometimes pull a small scam as a way to get food. While waiting at lunch counters for some busy man or woman to leave behind a cup of coffee and a partially eaten donut or meal, Lucy would sweep into their seat and ask for a refill on the coffee, pretending to be the original patron, as she'd devour their leftovers.

Determined to become a star, Lucille Ball ran into a bit of luck in 1933 when an agent decided her Chesterfield ads were good enough for her to be given a shot as a Goldwyn Girl for a new Eddie Cantor movie. Actually, the real luck was that the first chosen twelfth girl had backed out and Lucy became the second choice fill-in. She soon found her life a whirlwind of change as she was packed onto the Super Chief Train from New York to Hollywood.

# *1933-1939*
## *Lucy's First Visits to Palm Springs*

PALM SPRINGS WAS already five years into its Golden Age when Lucille Ball arrived in Southern California. Half a decade earlier, in 1928, the El Mirador hotel had completed construction and the numerous national celebrities well entrenched at its poolside rendezvous had transformed the little cowboy town into a haven for noteworthy guests. The Desert Inn was in full swing too and some of the earliest ranch style and Spanish Colonial homes were beginning to grow into a neighborhood of their own in what would fifty years later become known as the historic hotel district, snuggled just west of downtown in the afternoon shadow of Mount San Jacinto.

Hollywood had discovered the little village and was quietly enjoying the six beautiful months of the desert termed "prime season."

In Lucille Ball's first year in motion pictures (1933) she did four films. All of her parts were uncredited. But she was working. Her first initiations to Palm Springs would have been immediate upon setting foot onto the studio lots. Big wig producers, directors and A-list actors were commonly weekending in Palm Springs or taking longer retreats to recuperate – elite themes amongst those stressed out over heavy careers. The lure of career advancement upon a young chorus girl would be enormous. In those

18

days, many up and comers got their roles via the casting couch," though there's no evidence to support Lucy ever taking this low path to stardom. Still, she must have had her offers and Palm Springs had many couches in many hotel rooms. She was young and beautiful and men were attracted. The lecherous suggestions must have been made. Who would not want a weekend alone with a vivacious wide-eyed doe in a sultry desert landscape? Lounging around a warm pool, room service, afternoon horseback rides to enjoy during the day, and fine dining, cabaret entertainment and dancing in the evenings. It would be quite a temptation. The discreet lure of Palm Springs was enormous and heady with reputation. Yet, it offered secrecy.

Just listen to the rumors that would have flown amongst the young ladies of the studio back lots:

"Producer Darryl Zanuck is said to have a top floor suite out there that costs hundreds of dollars a night."

"Johhny Weismuller (Tarzan star) is supposed to show off his gorgeous body all day doing spectacular diving expeditions into a pool bigger than a sound stage and last winter they put the tree under water in the deep end. Johnny hung all the ornaments himself while holding his breath."

"Mr. Goldwyn owns an estate with five bathrooms. Can you imagine? And he just lends it out to his best stars. I hear Clark Gable wakes up in the mornings with a different girl each night, then takes a new one riding (horseback) each day."

"Last year, I heard Einstein spent an entire month there. Einstein! Can you believe it? And that man's smart. If he likes Palm Springs then it's gotta be a great place. Plus, I hear it's good for the complexion."

These rumors were not pure speculation either. Palm Springs was very much a happening lifestyle.

Outdoor athletics, swimming, tennis, riding, these

were the things you did when otherwise not leisurely enjoying being pampered. The hotel and tourism promoters were doing their best to attract America's elite and they were good at it. So good in fact, that the same people who would originally be guests at the hotels would eventually become homeowners themselves. From just Lucy's first four films after arriving in 1933, the moguls of Hollywood listed below would have been more than just idle conversation with their intent to make Palm Springs a part of their lives.

*The Bowery* – Actor George Raft was known to race his expensive convertible out to the desert and stay at the hotels. His co-star Jackie Cooper would go at times too. Cooper eventually purchased not just one home, but two there, as his growing career would allow him to upgrade his status and neighborhood. Director Raoul Walsh used *The Bowery* to further his career and eventually directed *Thief of Baghdad, High Sierra* and more. Walsh was one of the first to buy a home in Palm Springs, a luxurious 3,100sf private estate in 1937 in the desirable Movie Colony neighborhood.

*Broadway Through a Keyhole* – Producer William Goetz, who was Louis B. Mayer's son-in-law and would become Head of Production at both Universal and 20th Century Fox, signed a long-term lease for an estate in the Movie Colony, virtually a block from The El Mirador Hotel.

**Producers Darryl F. Zanuck and Joseph Schenck** would share a home in Palm Springs after a tax-evasive poker game allowed the title to change hands. They also become partners at 20th Century Fox which they created after buying and merging both 20th century Pictures and William F. Fox's studios.

*Roman Scandals* - Stage and film entertainer Eddie Can-tor was known to come to the desert often. By 1941, he and his wife Ida owned a 3 bedroom, 3 bath, 1,618sf Spaish Hacienda style home at 720 East Paseo El

Mirador.

Any one of these men, or more, could have introduced Lucy to Palm Springs. The best of Hollywood were wintering here, bringing friends, wives and consorts and remaking the desert into an oasis of relaxation and debauchery. It was far enough away from the prying eyes of the media and was unofficially considered a hands-off location for tabloid journalism, at least in the beginning. If a young actress were to accept an invitation from the right well-connected man, her career could shoot to the top.

So, in considering this, and as far as my research could reveal, let me share what I found on the young Miss Ball's Palm Springs introduction:

One of her first admirers and mentors in Hollywood was a young, 30 year old, director named Pandro S. Berman. Pandro, or Pan—as he was called—was married. He and Lucille would rendezvous at his apartment near RKO studio in Culver City, CA. Pan loved film production and was known to discuss such filmography elements as the transition of scenes or the flow of scripts in great detail. Though, despite other biographers claims that Pandro was affectionate with Lucy (now 24), she remained more of a pal than a lover with Pan. For his part, Berman cast Lucy in several films, one of which was *I Dream Too Much* (1935) where she played an American bleach-blonde gum chewer in Paris. Her one line was "Culture makes my feet hurt," a line she delivered with melodramatic comedic flair.

Pandro was known to visit Palm Springs in these days and eventually bought a 5 bedroom, 5 bath, 2,576sf house which was built in 1945 in the Mesa area. So far his ownership can only be verified as of 1951.

There is also the simple possibility she came out here with a girlfriend as Betty Grable and Joan Crawford did when sharing a room together at The Racquet Club. She would have probably taken a not so subtle hint from her number one female mentor, Carole Lombard, to be seen in Palm Springs rubbing elbows with "The Boys," as Lombard would have called the studio bosses. This type of hobnobbing would be of sincere benefit to Lucy's career in general. Lucy would have listened to Lombard too. She admired the platinum blonde for both her beauty and brazen attitude. And though this scenario is speculation, I believe another man she dated was most likely the actual first to bring her to the desert: Alexander Hall.

Hall was an up and coming director at the time of Ball's entry into Hollywood. In 1934, he directed *Little Miss Marker,* starring Shirley Temple (early El Mirador Hotel guest) and Adolphe Menjou (Las Palmas neighborhood homeowner). He had also been recently married (1934-36), and divorced from Lola Lane, a theatrical and movie actress, and he was in no hurry to remarry. Furthermore, he had friends: Charlie Ruggles, a veteran actor with a twenty year list of credits; Buster Keaton, a silent film star who'd made the transition into talkies; and Bill and Mary Gargan. Bill was a rising star with only four years more experience than Lucy. Yet, Bill had already accumulated an impressive list of credits.

Ball claimed Alexander Hall, Charlie Ruggles, Buster Keaton, and Bill and Mary Gargan, made a family of friends who did things together. She and Al were often seen about town. Lucy enjoyed Al's companionship and advice, but was not overly emotionally attached to him and neither made demands of each other. It was the perfect uncommitted relationship. It was relaxed. Perhaps this was true. Hall was twenty years her senior. But this was Hollywood and younger women often dated older men.

In the next chapter you'll read the proof of Alexander Hall's having stronger feelings for Lucy than she had for him. But, for now, accept as proof of Hall's love for Palm Springs, I submit his ritzy Las Palmas neighborhood residence, which is verified to be owned by the then seasoned director Hall in 1952. It's a 5 bedroom, 4 baths, 3,326sf home on an 11,761sf lot. Many of Palm Springs celebrity residents bought homes in their later years, having first been vacationers, as a way of reminiscing on their more boisterous youth and flamboyant times in the desert. Hall was most likely just such a man.

In 1938, Lucy played a credited role in *Room Service*, a Marx Brothers film. Groucho Marx had a reputation for sleeping with his starlets and in the first edition of this book, titled (slightly longer) P.S. I Love Lucy: The Story of Lucille Ball in Palm Springs, I further spread the rumor of the possibility of her being escorted to the desert by the mustachioed actor. But upon deeper investigation, I cannot find sufficient evidence to actively report this. It is merely rumor and not very likely. I am now unconvinced of a Groucho-Ball romantic affair. Though, in fairness, if she had, Lucy might have a gotten a Palm Springs residence sooner than she did. For in 1980, Groucho bought his then ex-wife, Eden Hartford, a Palm Springs 3 bedroom home at 1265 Serena Circle in the Movie Colony East neighborhood and Groucho did not meet Eden till much later in his life.

There was also a 1938 movie Lucy made, *Having a Wonderful Time* with Ginger Rogers (A verified resident of Palm Springs), who along with comic newcomer, Red Skelton (Long-time desert resident and Ball's comedic mentor), either of whom may have pointed Lucille Ball toward the desert playground.

Whether via Pandro S. Berman, Alexander Hall, Ginger Rogers, Red Skelton, Groucho Marx or merely with a girlfriend sharing a room, I can offer two pictures as the earliest evidence that Lucille Ball did come to Palm Springs in her young starlet days. The first is said to have been taken in one of the large trolley-style windows of the El Mirador Hotel in 1938. I used it on the cover of this book and again opposite the title page. The second, in the pages that follow, is taken at the El Mirador, on a set of outdoor steps, with Lucy wearing a large straw hat prior to 1940.

23

An aerial view of Palm Springs from the late 1930s. The two streets that run parallel to each other would be Indian Canyon Drive and Palm Canyon Drive. The building with the bell tower is the El Mirador Hotel. The neighborhood adjacent to the El Mirador is the Movie Colony. The area on the left of the photo is the Las Palmas neighborhood. Both neighborhoods are virtually unbuilt at this time, as in downtown in the bottom riight of the photo. This was Palm Springs, as it was, during Lucille Ball's first visits.

Lucille Ball on some steps at the El Mirador Hotel, circa 1940. It is autographed to a Mrs. MacManus. Pearl MacManus was one of the early founding mothers of Palm Springs.

Lucille Balll played the role of Christine in the 1938 Marx
Brothers film *Room Service*. Top to bottom: Harpo Marx,
Ann Miller, Zeppo Marx, Lucille Ball and Groucho Marx.

# 1940-1943
## Enter Desi Arnaz

LUCY SAW DESI for the first time at a New York Broadway play titled *Too Many Girls*, a prophetic name to their relationship, if ever there was one. She found him handsome in his hip hugging, shoulder swaying football player stage costume. His thick Latin accent only made him more desirous. She wanted to meet him. When she and a friend went to the nightclub Desi was performing at after the show, it was his night off. Lucy would have to wait.

Months later, between sets at RKO studios, she finally got her introduction.

Desi saw her first. Lucy was now wearing a burlesque queen costume from her film *Dance, Girl Dance*; a gold lame' dress slit up her thigh to the hip and she had a black eye because the scene called for fight between Lucy and Maureen O'Hara. Her shoulder-length hair had finally been dyed red but was mussed up causing Lucy to appear as a physically beaten harlot. Desi was at the commissary with director George Abbot, who introduced them, explaining Lucy was to play a small part in *Too Many Girls*. Desi thought Lucy wrong for the part. Abbott defended Lucy, saying if she was in the right costume and make-up she'd be perfect.

It wasn't till later in the day that they finally had anything resembling a real conversation. Lucy had changed to tight fitting beige slacks and a yellow sweater, and her hair was now dyed blonde and tied back in a bow. Desi was practicing the song, "She Could Shake the Maracas," with his piano player and didn't recognize her. So, they had to be introduced all over again. When Desi saw Lucy, he said "Man, what a honk (hunk) of a woman." To make up for his not recognizing her, she teased Desi by calling him Dizzy until he refuted. Then she called him Daisy. He carefully pronounced and spelled it for her: D-E-S-I. He offered her Rumba lessons and invited her to dinner. She accepted.

That night, they went to a nightclub, stared into each other's eyes and talked and talked, like young lovers do. She fell in love with Desi in five minutes—less. She loved looking at him and the only thing better than that, was listening to him speak.

His full name was Desidero Alberto Arnaz y de Ancha III. His father was a Doctor of Pharmacology who had been Mayor of Santiago, Cuba and owned ranch estates and city townhouses. His mother was a local beauty and heir to the Bacardi fortune. At only sixteen, Desi had owned both a car and a speedboat. Then the revolution came and they were driven from an island paradise to live a life of hard work in Miami, Florida. Within a few years he'd turned to music as a way to earn money and had started a Latin band. He'd been given a break by big band leader Xavier Cugat and soon Desi was playing dinner houses and night clubs. Then, he'd been discovered and offered the part in *Too Many Girls* on Broadway and when RKO bought the rights to the play, they'd wanted him to come to Hollywood.

Lucy spent the next few months showing Desi all her favorite spots around California. He'd come up a bit again since his laborious Miami days and once again owned a nice sports car. Together, they raced up and down the coast in Desi's black Buick Roadmaster convertible, exploring beaches, mountains (Big Bear) and Palm

Springs. When the road was open, they sped at over 100 miles an hour with the top down, enjoying Desi's most prized possession at the time—he had his initials painted in gold on the door—and, with their suitcases filled with her vivid Mandarin dresses and frilly nightgowns and his silk pajamas. Until she gained in Desi's driving, he scared the hell out of her. When Lucy did finally trust Desi behind the wheel she would stand up and scream full blast, letting the wind blow wild in her face. He asked her what she was doing and Lucy responded that Katherine Hepburn had told her to lower her voice and that the best way to do it was to scream while driving in an open car.

She screamed. He drove.

Where they stayed is unknown. But what is known is that their weekends would end with her begging him to stay and him saying he was doing the honorable thing by leaving. Not long after their romance began the other women riding in his passenger seat; Betty Grable, Gene Tierney, Lana Turner and other rising starlets, disappeared.

Likewise, soon after they started dating, Lucy called up Alexander Hall and broke off their seeing each other. Though Lucy claimed them to only be friends, Hall must have had stronger feelings. Upon being told that their relationship was over, one story told around the studio water cooler claimed Hall had a turkey delivered to her as a parting gift.

Desi's next movie, *A Girl, A Guy and a Gob*, was produced by Harold Lloyd, another Lucille Ball mentor, who owned a 5 bedroom, 6 bathroom, 7,006sf Palm Springs estate, at 899 North Avenida de Las Palmas, which he had built in the Movie Colony in 1925.

By November of 1940, Desi and Lucy found themselves deeply in love. Lucy wanted a strong man in her life and Desi wanted a family. Yet, Desi had a reputation for living life large and for the moment. Even with his reputation for cheating, drinking and staying out late, Lucy kept taking him back. She loved him for the best he was, a talented entertainer, and a man of strong convictions. Despite their love, they decided the difficulty of having two very busy Hollywood careers was incompatible to marriage. At the time, Desi was in New York, leading two bands at two different clubs; The Roxy and The Versailles, while Lucy had to go off to Milwaukee for a benefit show. Plus, they each had various other celebrity commitments which took them near and far throughout the country. One night, late, while in Wisconsin, Desi's hot temper flared and he called Lucy, accusing her of sleeping with actor Joseph Cotten, which was untrue. Despite his nasty accusations, she told Desi she'd see him first thing in the morning, back in New York.

Once back in The Big Apple, Desi told Lucy they were eloping. With his band manager driving, they sped to Greenwich, Connecticut and were wed after a brief confusion. Desi had forgotten the ring and had to run into Woolworth's to purchase one. Also, the Justice of the Peace changed the venue from the County Hall to the Byram River Beagle Club. They were wed and sped back to New York for Desi's show. Due to the news of their marriage spreading ahead of them via radio and the dangerous high-speed driving of Desi's manager, they still arrived a little late for Desi's show; but were welcomed by a standing ovation of the night club's most crowded night yet. People were literally spilling into the street for a peek at the new bride and groom.

Desi had a contract with RKO to do movies six months of the year. So, he could travel with his band the other six. This routine often brought long separations between him and Lucy. They were constantly jealous of each other and who the other might be with. They'd call each other a couple times a day and on many of those days, at least one of the calls would end with a shouting match and a hang-up. Leading to the makeup calls. Sometimes, Desi would even go so far as to send Lucy a telegram. One in particular, which Desi sent from Knoxville, Tennessee after a particularly nasty phone fight, expressed his regrets about the fight and how much loved her. He said how he missed her, very much and expressed concern for losing his head. He said how much he enjoyed talking to her. But, he felt awful when he had to hang up. Then he went on to say how he hoped to see her in Palm Springs and then wished her love.

In tying together dates from their biographies, Love Lucy (Berkley Publishing, 1997, page 105) and A Book (William, Morrow, and Company, Inc., 1976, page 129), it seems that after a particular Palm Springs trip Desi met Lucy's Grandfather for the first time, Fred C. Hunt. Because of the Palm Springs sun and Desi's Cuban olive skin tone, Desi was very tan and after being introduced, Lucy's Grandfather pulled her aside and expressed the concern that though he thought Desi a nice young man, Grandpa Hunt felt the Cuban to be a little dark.

In April of 1942, Desi joined the Hollywood Victory Caravan, made up of some twenty-plus Hollywood stars and starlets to tour nationally on behalf of Army and Navy Relief. Desi got top billing because his last name started with an A, otherwise he would not have. The list of entertainers included (alphabetically): Joan Bennett, Joan Blondell, Charles Boyer, James Cagney, Jerry Colonna, Claudette Colbert, Olivia de Havilland, Cary Grant, Charlotte Greenwood, Bob Hope, Bert Lahr, Frances Langford, Laurel and Hardy, Groucho Marx, Frank McHugh, Ray Middleton, Pat O'Brien, Merle Oberon, Eleanor Powell, and Rise Stevens. Bing Crosby later joined the group. This was an embarrassing time for Lucy as studio rumors and tabloids depicted Desi chasing every available skirt on the tour.

Also in 1942, Lucille Ball took on three projects to keep herself busy: *The Big Street*, with Henry Fonda, where she played a bitch who abuses the admiration of a young man; *Seven Days' Leave,* in which she played an heiress who Victor Mature must marry to inherit $100,000; and she began production of a movie which would cement a friendship between her and Red Skelton that would last a lifetime. Though they had performed together four years earlier in *Having a Wonderful Time,* their respect for each other grew as they co-starred together in *DuBarry was a Lady.* In *DuBarry,* Lucy proved she could carry a musical comedy and found a respect for Red's poignant humor and sadness.

Years later, Skelton would help her develop a vaudevillian comedy routine using clown-like shtick so she and Desi could perform on stage together. He would also purchase a home near theirs in Rancho Mirage. Skelton's home, at 37801 Thompson Road in Tamarisk Country Club, had a superb Japanese garden which Red had enriched with some $80,000 in landscaping. Lucy admired Red's ability to train and prune the trees himself with expert skill and knew that Red would often enjoy his teahouse on clear desert nights, embracing Haiku music and looking up at San Jacinto Mountain like it was his own personal Mount Fuji.

Lucy sometimes mentioned Red couldn't even buy a house in a conventional way. He'd bought his Rancho Mirage home after one of his golfing buddies offered to show him his home. Skelton was there in his bare feet and trunks only a few minutes before offering to buy it for cash, with one condition: The current owner and his family had to move out that same afternoon. Red then pulled $135,000 out of his bathing trunks, they shook hands, and the deal was made.

Unlike Lucy's popular film career – she was now consistently playing leading ladies and having her pick of projects – Desi was better known as a musician than an actor. His films had been only warmly received and his recognition around Hollywood was somewhat lackluster. The studio bosses were more and more often comparing him to another Latin up comer, Ricardo Montalban, who Desi lost a few parts to because of Montalban's clearly enigmatic voice.

One night, when going out for the evening, Desi became highly insulted when at the end of the night the couple went out to get their car. The valet looked them up and down, then shouted, "Bring up Miss Ball's car!"

Lucy understood. Desi wanted to stand on his own. But, his star was not rising as fast as hers even though he had even had achieved his most critically acclaimed best performance yet in a movie called *Bataan*, where he played one of a handful of soldiers on a South Pacific island (shot in St. Thomas), each telling their tale of home and war before being picked off one after the other by Japanese snipers. Acclaimed? Yes. Career changing? No.

Ironically, at 26 years old, in May of 1943, Desi got drafted. He was still not a U.S. citizen. To fast track citizenship, he'd tried to enlist a few years earlier. Though, at the time, he was rejected on grounds of not being a citizen, the laws allowed for him to be drafted. And, drafted he was.

Unfortunately, the day before he was to leave he injured his knee in a baseball game. He still went through Basic Training, where he had a few fights over his heritage and celebrity status, and then was offered a position entertaining the troops at home, mostly in California. With Lucy's help, they enlisted a lot of other stars: Ann Sheridan, Lana Turner, Tommy Dorsey, and his orchestra, Mickey Rooney, Lena Horne, Martha Raye and more. One of his most successful strategies was getting a lot of the pretty girls from the studios to serve cold milk to patient soldiers in a psychological rehabilitation unit at Birmingham Hospital in the San Fernando Valley. Due to the amount of losses going on in the South Pacific at the time, there were a lot of casualties and the number one thing a returning G.I. would ask for was a glass of cold milk. Having a lot of young beauties to serve it to the injured men went a long way towards welcoming the injured soldiers back home.

Desi did a lot of good. He even funded a movie theatre for the troops and cunningly surpassed the red tape, which until Desi got involved, was blocking the project. He also tells a great little tale of helping an angry returning G.I. turn his bad attitude into a positive force while calling Bingo numbers with band leader Eddie LeBaron.

But…, but…

But, Desi was still not coming home enough to Lucy at night, even when he was stationed very close by and the rumors of his off base exploits were reaching Lucy's ears. Though Desi would deny them, where there was smoke, Lucy sensed fire.

Lucy had just finished making a film with Katharine Hepburn and Spencer Tracy called *Without Love*, and despite Desi's protestations, Lucy was justified in her convictions to challenge him. She just couldn't prove it. Though, she was definitely right.

The following is an excerpt from <u>Confidential Magazine</u>, which wasn't published till a decade later in January of 1954. It details a Palm Springs weekend of Desi's in October 1944 and shows exactly what kind of distant husband he was at the time.

"He (Desi) was an army sergeant stationed in Birmingham Hospital in Van Nuys at the time. Because he had plenty of money, his week-end leaves were something special and included a private room at the Del Tahquitz Hotel in Palm Springs. (South-east corner of Baristo and Palm Canyon Drive, no longer standing. It was torn down in 1960 to make room for a Santa Fe Savings and Loans).

"Desi met our dark-eyed temptress, Sally, in the cocktail lounge of the Ambassador Hotel and asked both her and her girl friend to join his table, which included several other men and a few women. Before the excitement hunting babes knew what happened, they found themselves at a party in the home of an army officer stationed in Palm Springs.

"The girl recalls she spent the next five or six hours smooching and drinking with Desi. She noted one of Desi's eyes was extremely bloodshot. When she asked him whether he'd injured the orb, Mr. Arnaz explained he'd been born with his hangover glitter.

"Hours later, they paused for a little air and light conversation, during which Sally asked Desi about the break-up marriage. The Arnaz smile vanished and he scowled, "This marrying for love is the bunk." The girl remembers that Desi was obviously a man carrying a torch but she was, too, at the time, so they agreed to drown their sorrows together.

"Long after dawn had risen, she accepted Arnaz' invitation for a nightcap at his hotel. His request, incidentally, was a request other wolves might study.

"Let's have a couple of drinks at my place," he said. "Better bring your bathing suit along. We might want to go swimming when we wake up."

"I knew Desi was inviting me for more than a drink," said the babe. "I said okay, because I can make like the outdoor type, too, when the occasion calls for it."

"They drove to Sally's hotel for the swimsuit, and she rushed in and out of the place so fast that she tore a heel off her shoe. It didn't bother the frisky filly in the least. Grabbing her bikini, she didn't wait to change shoes but dashed back into the car and was soon limping through the lobby of the Del Tahquitz, to the astonishment of the night clerk."

"On their way to the elevator and their early-morning amour, they met still another girl friend of Sally's, a Latin, incidentally, with whom Desi immediately struck up a brisk conversation in Spanish. She was invited to join them."

"The extra girl went along but got out of there fast when she quickly realized two's company, three's a crowd."

"Hours later, Sally limped back to her own hotel and her week-end pal. To her, Sally sighed one rapturous comment: "Who ever said Latins are lousy lovers?" she asked drowsily."

"Who, indeed? Certainly not Desi's wife, Lucy. For in spite of his straying from the hearth, she loves him dearly."

"And Desi most certainly loves Lucy. It's just that, like a lot of other husbands, he's got a little extra – to go around."

# 1944-1949
## Breaking Up is Hard to Do

THE MARRIAGE WAS a continual rocky balancing act. The two barely stayed together until after Lucy's grandfather, Fred C. Hunt, died in January, 1944. She had had enough and Lucy filed for divorce. But in the fall of 1944, at Desi's request, Lucy went to see him on the eve of their fourth wedding anniversary while she was en route to pick up the final divorce decree. They had dinner together and while doing so revisited all the best and worst points of their marriage. In the end, they both shared the things they'd do differently the next time they wed. So Desi said something to the effect, 'Why let others benefit from our mistakes? Let's make those corrections now for each other and give ourselves another shot.' Lucy agreed and they sealed their pact with a love making session and the divorce was never finalized.

By 1945, at the age of 34, Lucy's popularity had dipped a little due to a mild reception of her movie *Without Love*, Desi's ever more publicized indiscretions and the tempestuous, yet uncompleted divorce. It seemed fans were more ready for her to go her own way rather than stay with the philandering Cuban. But, Lucy loved Desi, and stay she did. Like many women of her day, may people, she chose love over career. Lucy put on blinders to Desi's shenanigans and for his part; Desi came home at night.

Both were trying to make it work. Palm Springs became their playground even though it was the place where Desi's lack of judgment had hurt the relationship, Lucy didn't know yet of that particular indiscretion – it wouldn't be printed for nine more years. The two were seen around town arm in arm, playing tennis at The Racquet Club, dining together, dancing and enjoying life.

When Desi got out of the military in late 1945, he started up an orchestra and with the help of Walter Krasner. They drew from the best of the heavy rhythm of Latin bands and blended in the melodic sounds of Andre Kostelanetz, which was "lush" but had, as Desi put it, "No Balls." The orchestra packed Ciro's in Hollywood and placed the Cuban back on the map and forefront in the minds of Hollywood big wigs.

Then their careers took over again and Desi, now 28, was travelling with his Orchestra around the country, while Lucy was working on projects at the studio. Their old routines were hard to break.

That same year, Lucy filmed her part of a movie that was almost prophetic of things to come. *Ziegfield Follies* was a medley of musical and comedy skits with an ensemble cast based on the Broadway show of the same name. In it, William Frawley (Fred Mertz) played a wary landlord with a crafty wife and Lucy's old Palm Springs friend, Red Skelton, portrayed a very funny drunken radio announcer that was practically a premonition to the Vitameatavegamin skit; yet to come.

Unfortunately, Lucy's career was stagnating once again. Her contract with MGM was close to expiring and although her last few films were good, they were not received with the sort of fanfare complementary to an A-list film career. On the other hand, Desi's orchestra was doing well. As a whole though, they had money and were closer than ever. However, what they really wanted was to work together and to have a family.

Lucy and Desi were anxious to try and coordinate their careers into a lifestyle that would allow them to spend more time together. Lucy approached another Palm Springs friend, Bob Hope, with the concept of Desi and his Orchestra performing for Hope's very popular radio show. The biggest problem was that by the time Lucy convinced Bob to use Desi there were only two days to get the band to Hollywood from Omaha, Nebraska. Lucy's brother Fred was the band manager at the time and the best he could do was to hire a produce pilot of the Midwest Vegetable Co. to load the band into his plane alongside bushels of lettuce. After a long delay due to fog and a brief return to Omaha because a propeller quit turning, the band finally made it as far west as the California desert where the pilot asked for directions. He'd never been this far west before. Luckily, Desi recognized the lights of Palm Springs below them. He had flown in, out and over the city enough times to know the village by sight and with the help of the Los Angeles Airport Tower, Desi was able to navigate their way visually the rest of the way home with only one small correction to their course. They were told to increase their altitude by 2,000 feet due to the mountains in the area. Wise advice! Thirty years later these same mountains would take the lives of Dean Martin's son, Frank Sinatra's mother, and Palm Springs father and son home-builder team, George and Robert Alexander, in three separate plane crashes.

When the going gets tough, the tough get going.

Desi considered the time he spent working for Bob Hope his finest education in the art of comedy and production. He was personally being tutored by the best professor: Mr. Bob Hope. As Musical Director, Desi would sit in on development meetings for Hope's show. In the writers meeting he'd watch Bob collect twelve different full-length written scripts into his office and spread them out on the floor while, at Bob's direction, secretaries with tape and scissors would cut and paste the best parts from each into an entirely new and better show. Desi would also get to know who that week's guest star was going to be and watched how Bob fitted them into the show with jokes, sketches and music. Then Desi would be part of the rehearsals that week, with the shows regulars – Jerry Colonna, Vera Vague, etc., - as they prepared for the real show, which was performed in front of a live audience. Desi also would interview the ever-changing weekly hottie girl who would be part of Bob's show. Desi credits himself with discovering Doris Day, who he chose because of her sexy derriere. Other than finding Day though, Desi credits Bob with supervising every facet of the show, from supervising to producing and directing it. On the night of the show, Hope would walk onstage to the tune of "Thanks for the Memories," and take over the audience like no one else ever could. The most amazing thing to Desi was how, after all this work, Bob would tell the punch lines to jokes as if they weren't even funny, yet the audience was roaring with laughter.

There was one other thing Desi saw Bob Hope do that he thought was extremely smart. Hope could turn on and off his entertainers' persona like a light switch. When Bob was onstage and the cameras were rolling, he was energetic, effervescent, and overflowing; full of pep and vigor. Yet, when the lights and music were off, Hope had the ability to unplug and relax. It was like turning on or off a motor. To Desi, this was a great talent.

This ability to turn the Hollywood persona on and off was Desi's one criticism of Lucy. She did not have the ability to put on those mental and physical brakes. She would often bring her work home with her and worry about her script, her acting, the studio. The very thing that made Lucy great, her concentrated effort, also caused stress. And though she was awesome in her performances, Desi wished at times she could turn off her Hollywood persona and they could just be Lucy and Desi.

Back to Bob Hope: for all Bob and Desi's good work together, there was one time when Hope got mad at Desi. It happened when Al Jolson, a popular comedic singer, did Hope's radio show. Bob strictly told Desi not to let the applause continue on when Jolson took the stage. Rather, Desi was to start right into a song after Hope's introduction. But, before the show, Jolson pulled Desi aside and told him not to start the music till Jolson turned to him and said, "Maestro."

Desi followed Jolson's advice and allowed him to soak up several precious minutes of Hope's half hour show. Jolson's ability to charm the audience into continued clapping was amazing to Desi and out of the corner of his eye he could see Hope cussing him out in several languages.

After the show, Hope confronted Desi about it and Desi played dumb and asked, "...wouldn't that have stopped the applause...?" 'Bob looked at him and with that beautiful, humorous, sarcastic expression of his and said, "R-E-A-L-L-Y?"' As Hope walked away, he turned back over his shoulder and called, "You shit!"

While Desi was getting his education from Bob Hope, Lucy was getting an education of her own. Just before leaving MGM, she was loaned out to 20th Century Fox to do a show called *The Dark Corner*, with Mark Stevens, Clifton Webb, and William Bendix. During that time, she was so stressed out that she started stuttering. The pressures of her marriage, stagnating career and being childless, it was all just too much. The Director of *The Dark Corner* didn't help either. He began berating Lucy on set, even accused her of drinking. What was worse, she found out that her agent and the studio were making an unfairly large amount of money on her being loaned out for the picture. She felt over-stressed, over-worked and underappreciated.

Her agent was unsympathetic. She wanted to fire him. The only way out of her contract with him was to quit

MGM. So, that's what she did. However, the act of quitting did not alleviate the stress; because, now she was unemployed.

When one door closes, another one opens. A new well-known agent, Kurt Frings, showed up on her doorstep and though there is some discrepancy over whether or not Olivia de Haviland (a woman Lucy greatly respected) sent him – Lucy says yes, the agent says no. Either way, the man turned out to be a saving angel. He convinced Lucy to free-lance and even had a picture lined up for her, *Lover Come Back*, with Universal, directed by Bill Seiter. Bill turned out to be a charming man who re-inspired Lucy's confidence. The movie was largely panned by critics. But, for Lucy, it was exactly what she needed to reignite her attitude.

It was 1946, WWII was over, and Hollywood was having its biggest year ever. Desi was playing the best clubs and doing Bob Hope's show and Lucy was enjoying the success of several movies at once. Still, she wasn't climbing as high as she wanted and felt her career was lackluster. So, she switched to theatre and, in 1947, Lucy found herself performing *Dream Girls* around the country. Desi claims these were some of the worst years of their marriage. Both he and Lucy were travelling all the time, hardly seeing each other, and when they did it would often climax into either a mad love making session or one hell of a fight.

Tragedy struck. When Lucy was in Detroit, performing *Dream Girls*, Desi and his band were in a bus wreck. The driver had fallen asleep at the wheel. Many of the band members were injured and one even lost an eye. A lawsuit would eventually compensate the half-blind member as much as money could. But most immediately, just as it looked like the rest of the tour was going to have to be cancelled, some of Desi's fiercest band competitors saved the day. Xavier Cugat, Duke Ellington, and Tommy Dorsey, flew in musicians to fill the injured ranks. The band played on.

Though Desi was the spouse with the reputation for philandering infidelities, there was one time when Lucy may have been the unfaithful one. With Desi gone many months of the year, it would have been simple for her to step out on him and he often accused her of it in their frantic phone calls to each other, Lucy fanned the fires pretending to be spending time with someone else as a way of getting even with Desi. But, when she made the United Artists movie *Lured*, and was introduced to her co-star George Sanders, a six-foot-three Englishman who towered over Lucille's five foot seven frame, her farcical trysts may have shifted into reality. Sanders had a comforting presence, light brown hair and an uncanny appreciation for art and music. Between takes, George's gray-green eyes held Lucy's steadily and he would do something no man had ever done before. He listened when Lucy talked. He was a competent English gentleman who tossed about flattery like it was daisies. He was worldly. He was charming.

Sanders was married at the time he met Lucy, but according to his future wife, Zsa Zsa Gabor, that didn't preclude the two from having an affair. Before she and George were married, Zsa Zsa was having an affair with George at the same time as Lucy too; while she was still married to Conrad Hilton. Zsa Zsa became suspicious of George and Lucy when one time she called George and in the background of the phone conversation Zsa Zsa could hear Lucy demanding, "What are you doing with that Hilton woman? You know that I love you. She's too young for you!"

Lucy may or may not have been indiscrete though. She always claimed to have been faithful to Desi. And, while George may have been a player, he eventually wed Zsa Zsa in a marriage that lasted from 1949 to 1954. In 1970, George also wedded and bedded Zsa Zsa's sister Magda Gabor. But that marriage only lasted six months due to George's excessive drinking.

George Sanders may have also been Lucy's inspiration. Shortly after Lucy's dalliance with George, Lucy had enough of the long distance relationship with Desi. They both committed to try even harder to make it work. For her part, Lucy footed much of the bill to move *Dream Girls* from Detroit to Los Angeles. She even paid extra so many of the younger, newer and less fortunate membersof the cast could be seen in a city that might actually matter to their careers. Yet before they got there, many of the members grew ill and the show never got off the ground.

In 1949, Lucy and Desi remarried in a Catholic church as a way to rededicate their love in the eyes of God. Lucy had never really felt as if they were married, since their first wedding was performed by a Justice of the Peace. The two remarried at Our Lady of the Valley Church in Canoga Park with a small ceremony of only the closest family and friends. Now, with the ceremony steeped in religious conviction, the two could believe their vows to be an ordained truth and they were more determined than ever to make it work. They sought only one more blessing. Unfortunately, that year Lucy miscarried and though the doctor told them, 'It was for the best.' They were despondent over the lost child.

Lucy took to radio as a means of furthering her entertainment career while solidifying her family goals. Hollywood was in a downward spiral and the movie studios were cutting back due to big losses in the film industry. Radio allowed for a steady home life; a fact proven by the stable marriages of Mr. and Mrs. Jack Benny, George Burns and Gracie Allen, and Ozzie and Harriet Nelson. Lucy wanted Desi to play her spouse with her on a husband and wife show. But, CBS said no and instead Lucy did a series called *My Favorite Husband* with Richard Denning about a wacky wife who does crazy things to promote her husband's banking career.

Also In 1949, for greater privacy, Lucy and Desi instituted a stay-at-home policy and got rid of the hanger's on around the San Fernando Valley, Chatsworth ranch house, which they'd started calling Desilu Ranch. For his part, Desi decided he would no longer tour across the country with the band, only contracting local engagements, and in their ongoing efforts to conceive, each would consult a doctor to see if there was anything wrong with either of them that prevented them physically from having a baby.

Their careers were stable and poised to move forward. Lucy signed a contract with Columbia Pictures for a movie, as did Desi; even though Desi was already in high demand in the Los Angeles area, making some $12,000 a week with his orchestra and simultaneously doubling as Bob Hope's Music director. Lucy's radio show was popular and the studios were calling again. The family life at home was pleasant and each wanted to be together. They were happy and the desire for children was stronger than ever.

Then Lucy found a new project with the help of her old friend Bob Hope. They were cast together in a movie called *Sorrowful Jones* and every day she found going to his set was like going to a party. He helped her hone her comedy. She enjoyed working with Bob so much; she made a second film with him, *Fancy Pants*. It was nearly 1950 and Lucy was turning 39 years old. She'd been working as an actress since she was 14 and she finally felt as if she'd arrived in Hollywood. Directors and Producers were even talking about roles with the phrase, 'A Lucille Ball type.'

It may have been Bob Hope who reignited Lucy's adventures in Palm Springs. Her leaner income years were fading into the past and Bob had owned a home in the desert for some ten years. Desi would've liked the idea. He had a secret past in the desert and was a man who would have dared to revisit it. All that's certain is that they were again seen together around Palm Springs. They did not yet have a home n the desert. But, The Racquet Club became a place for them to enjoy.

Other things were taking shape in their life too. Gale Gordon, who would, more than a decade later play Lucy's bank boss on *The Lucy Show,* was introduced to the radio cast of *My Favorite Husband* and in the show he was given a wife who became Lucy's female co-conspirator. Together they would connive and conspire to improve their lives through their husband's careers – a scenario that would go center stage for Lucy and Desi in their own show one day. Lucy was also bonding a great friendship with the writers Madelyn Pugh and Bob Carroll, Jr. The two were instrumental with the changes about to emerge in the soon to blossom Ball-Arnaz empire, as would the radio show's Producer-Director, Jess Oppenheimer.

The happy couple were a frequent sight at gatherings
in and around Palm Springs.

A beautiful wife and her handsome latin husband
sharing a romantic dance.

# 1950-1953
## Desilu Comes Into Focus

FOR LUCILLE BALL and Desi Arnaz, the desire to work together as a husband and wife team was a focal point in their lives. In the spring of 1950, true to their intentions, they decided to create Desilu Productions.

That year, CBS had been talking ever more seriously about transferring *My Favorite Husband* to television and Lucy became ever more forceful in her desire that Desi play her husband. She wanted to work with the man she loved and thought the show the perfect vehicle. CBS still didn't agree. They just didn't think the U.S. audiences were ready for a Cuban husband and a red-headed American girl as his wife.

Lucy and Desi were unfazed with the studio execs skepticism. Even though they knew there were risks, they decided to put together a travelling act to test their theatrical compatibility. They had a lot to lose if this didn't work. Lucy was now netting more than $100,000 a year in pictures and Desi's band was at a perceived zenith of popularity. Still, the desire to perform together was the most important thing in the world to them.

They called upon an old friend of Desi's to help them, Pepito Perez, "the Spanish Clown," to help Lucy put together her comedic pantomime part in the show and the great silent film star, director and producer, Buster Keaton, showed Lucy how to perform melodramatically with the cello. Desi would play himself really and be her straight man. Jess Oppenheimer produced their Vaudevillian show and the writers from *My Favorite Husband*, Bob Carroll, Jr. and Madelyn Pugh wrote the script. During the 1950's Carroll and Pugh would eventually end up working full time for the Arnazes.

In the act, Desi performed with his band, while Lucy was a hobo clown who wanted to be in the act, miming her skills by using a plunger as a bow. Desi was unnerved. Lucy showed further skills by playing a horn rack like a seal. Desi sang and danced to Cuban Pete. Lucy mimicked him by singing she was "Sally Sweet. The Queen of Delancey Street. Boom Chicky Boom." The crowd loved them and while test marketing themselves in these shows around the country, Lucy and Desi were jet setting back and forth to meet their other obligations of band performances and film industry deals.

The real problem to Lucy and Desi now was that Lucy was being offered generous movie roles and she was still under contract with Columbia. *The Fuller Brush Girl* fulfilled one of her two final contract pictures, but then Columbia Pictures President, Harry Cohn, was reluctant to let Lucy out of her contract. She was offered a role with Paramount Studios in Cecil B. DeMille's epic *The Greatest Show on Earth*, which she wanted desperately. To try and thwart her, Cohn offered her a deal breaker of a picture, a lousy class E film where she played a harem girl; *The Magic Carpet*. Cohn thought Lucy would refuse and he'd get out of her contract and not have to pay her. Instead, Lucy missed out on *The Greatest Show on Earth* and pretended to gush at the part in *The Magic Carpet* and Cohn was forced to pay her $85,000 for five days work. Plus, she was now free from Columbia and able to work with Desi.

She also had some suspicions she might be pregnant again.

In October, 1950, Desi and his Orchestra opened for the Chi Chi Club in Palm Springs. Lucy came along for several weeks as a break from the stress of trying to create her and Desi's own TV show. Their vaudeville performances were being widely accepted. The couple needed to strategize their next steps.

The Chi Chi was originally opened in 1931, when hotelier and Las Vegas casino owner Irwin Schuman converted The Waffle House into a dinner theatre. It was located in the heart of downtown at 217 North Palm Canyon Drive and packed in guests by the hundreds. It was a favorite watering hole of the stars and on any particular night there could be just as many celebrities in the audience as there were performing. On stage, you might see Nat King Cole, Liberace, Lena Horne, and more, and in the audience would be Sammy Davis, Jr., Bing Crosby, Dean Martin, Frank Sinatra, Eddie Cantor, and more. As a matter of fact, Sinatra supposedly met his second wife, Ava Gardner, at the Chi Chi Club one night when the emcee called out for a partner switch and Frank left his first wife, Nancy Barbato, behind while he was flung into the waiting arms of Ava.

When Irwin Schuman, who also owned The Riviera Resort in Las Vegas, wanted to hire Desi for The Chi Chi Club, it was a gig hard to turn down. Schuman would nearly a decade later (1959) build the Riviera Resort in Palm Springs. He had a great love for the desert. The Chi Chi would continue on till it was torn down in 1977. But in 1950 it was Palm Springs epicenter of quality entertainment.

So, the Arnazes came, played and stayed. Palm Springs offered them a chance to grow and reflect; a chance to perform and perfect, both their careers and their love for one another.

While Desi was performing at the Chi Chi Club, he ran into CBS's West Coast top gun, Harry Ackerman. Ackerman pitched the idea of a game show with Desi being the host. It was to be called *Tropical Vacation* and have three contestants competing for prize money with a two week trip to various Latin American destinations as the grand prize. An added bonus was that theOrchestra would perform too. Desi liked the theme of the show, even though after his costs, including paying the orchestra, there wouldn't be much left for him. It worked with his and Lucy's idea of 'No Touring.'

What really cemented Desi's doing the show was when, in November, the Arnazes doctor formally declared Lucy with child. Desi threw himself into production of the show and used his earnings to build a two room nursery onto the San Fernando Valley ranch home.

Lucy found herself in marriage bliss. Desi was the most attentive he had ever been to her. He doted on her, even driving his now yellow convertible at respectable speeds rather than roaring and racing across town or out to the desert on their getaway jaunts. The only thing amiss was that they still hadn't fulfilled their desire to work together.

Desi became the persistent one. Using his *Tropical Vacations* connections, he convinced CBS President, William S. Paley, to shoot the pilot for *I Love Lucy*. Negotiations were difficult. The sponsor, Phillip Morris, wanted the show shot in New York for the best film quality. In those days, all the top shows were shot there because the cross country TV cables had yet to be laid and to shoot on the West coast necessitated filming in Kinescope, which was blurry. Added to this mix was the fact that CBS and Phillip Morris insisted on a budgetary ceiling that they thought would force Lucy and Desi's hand. In a fit of desperation, or clarity – either of which could be true – Desi offered to pay for the extra expenses to shoot the TV show on movie quality film himself. However, there were three conditions: The first was that the show would be shot live in L.A.; the second was that Lucy and he would own the rights to the show; and lastly Desi would get a Producer billing. CBS and Phillip Morris agreed thinking the production costs would soon crush Desi and in the end the studio and sponsor would still get everything they wanted.

As *I Love Lucy* came closer to reality, Lucy became a Nervous Nellie. In those days, TV was the bane of movies and if the show flopped, finding work would be extremely difficult. On top of that risk, the costs financially enormous. It was a huge gamble. Lucy claimed one night she was steered towards the challenge ahead by a visionary dream of Carole Lombard, whereby Lombard urged her, "Go ahead. Give it a whirl."

From the very start, Lucy and Desi wanted a family show. Part of it would mirror their own life; including, featuring Desi as a bandleader. Initially, they tried a pilot with it exactly mirroring their lives, with Lucy being an actress on the edge of greatness and Desi a renowned bandleader. But, they quickly figured the show would be better accepted by the public if they played parts more viewers could associate with. They also determined that the humor would be good-natured – never mean or unkind. The characters of Lucy and Ricky were committed to each other, regardless of financial difficulties or flirtatious guests. Ricky would be a real man, who would never be portrayed as an idiot husband and if Lucy had a conspiratorial joke to drop on her husband, Ricky would be allowed to break the fourth wall and wink at the audience, so they knew he was in on the gag. In the end, they would always fall back into each other's arms, still madly, hopelessly, in love with each other. When Fred (William Frawley) and Ethel Mertz (Vivian Vance) were written in, it allowed for a men-versus-women element to the script, giving both Lucy and Desi co-conspirators in their never ending escapades.

The pilot was well received. Thirty-nine episodes were to be shot the first year and despite the difficulties of staging the live shooting of TV comedy, the new Desilu Productions, which Lucy and Desi formalized as their financial vehicle to produce the show, pulled it off. This involved renting a sound stage from RKO studios and customizing it to suit. More and more their lives were riding on the outcome of the *I Love Lucy* show.

It was early 1951 and Lucy's baby bubble was starting to bulge.

The first episode was to be shot after the baby was born. Nothing was more important to Lucy and Desi than the arrival of their first child. At 8:15 am, on July 17, 1951, Lucie Desiree Arnaz was born, weighing seven pounds, eight ounces. Less than a month shy of her own fortieth birthday, Lucille Ball was finally a mother.

Filming was set to begin in September and the rest was Hollywood history, a fantastic show was born. Desilu Studios became a major production company, developing new cameras, styles and capabilities for shooting in front of a live audience. Lucy and Desi became mega-stars and broke the old models of acceptability In interracial marriages. A new era dawned in American television, in American civilization. But, there is more.

In 1952, Desi made another of his smart business moves. He started a new company called Zanra (Arnaz backwards) which was an equipment rental business. It allowed him to do a neat and tricky accounting thing. Through Zanra, he was able to buy all the Desilu equipment at cost and then rent it back to his own company. What this meant was that CBS, who had a vested interest in the production of *I Love Lucy,* was denied a greater share of the profits. This didn't come out till the second season of the show, and not really until Desilu began producing its second show, called *Our Miss Brooks*, starring Eve Arden as a school teacher. This was the first of many mega-income years to come for Lucy and Desi. Zanra made more than $300,000 in equipment rentals that year and Desilu inked a deal with CBS for $1,000,000, plus there was the sponsorship of Phillip-Morris.

Shortly thereafter, due to their unique capability of filming live situational comedy, Desilu was making several shows. Some of the earliest were: *Letter to Loretta* starring Loretta Young, *The Danny Thomas Show*(s), T*he Ray Bolger Show*, and four of *The Jack Benny Show*(s).

As the couple's popularity grew to new heights, they sought a place to grant themselves a reprieve from the hustle and bustle of Hollywood. Palm Springs became that refuge. There are five places laying claim to Lucille Ball and Desi Arnaz staying there during the early 1950's. Lucy and Desi were back in Palm Springs and the only thing they really needed was a permanent place to call their own. In the fall of 1953 they began construction on just such a place. Three of them I'm unsure of. One seems absolutely false. They also had some business adventures in the desert. Let's explore some of these stories of their mid-life escapades in the desert:

The Ocotillo Lodge claims that Lucy and Desi stayed here while their home in the Thunderbird Country Club was being built. I find it hard to believe. I think the couple had better options available to them – as you'll see with the last claim – and, I suspect they would've sought a greater degree of privacy in their lives at this time than the Ocotillo could provide. It's a big property and even in its earliest times was a very public place. Then there's also the fact that the Ocotillo Lodge wasn't constructed till 1957 and Lucy and Desi's Thunderbird Country Club home was built in 1954.

Club Trinidad claims Lucy and Desi stayed in the penthouse suite while they were building their Thunderbird home. Though the penthouse is a 1,300sf, two bedroom second floor suite with a complete kitchen, the difficulty with this rumor is that the hotel opened in 1960 and Lucy and Desi's Thunderbird home was built in 1954. After discussing the issue with the hotel CEO and General Manager, he decidedly retracted the rumor, confirming it merely rumor passed down through generations of managers. Upon further inspection, he disclosed the hotel had a secluded card room and that, at times, employees of Desilu had stayed there. Both are possibilities. Ken Tobey, the star of Desilu's production *Whirlybirds* (1957-1960) had lived around the corner since 1951; thus making Palm Springs newest hotel, at the time, a much desired convenience. And, Desi did have a fondness for gambling and secret rendezvous destinations. Any of these theories could lead to a thread of truth. Unfortunately, there is no written record, no hotel registry book or copy of receipts exists to verify these possibilities.

Andalusian Court hotel is located at 458 W. Arenas Avenue in the Tennis Club neighborhood. It was built in 1922 and it was owned by the Sinclair family and called The El Poco Lodge. It's rumored to have been a favorite spot for Lucy and Desi to stay during the 1940s and 1950s. While it's been claimed that they stayed here during construction of their Thunderbird Country Club house – a recurring theme amongst hotel owners in Palm Springs – I again find that premise unlikely. It's more likely that they stayed here during their times they wanted greater privacy on many of their getaway weekends or during 1950 when Desi and his orchestra headlined at the Chi Chi Club's Starlight Room. At the time, the buildings were amongst a very few in the neighborhood and with the way the pool was nestled between an office and a two-story structure they would have been nicely secluded. The rumors of the Arnazes staying in unit four include this being a favorite spot for the couple to stay immediately after the birth of Desi, Jr. It's claimed the littlest Arnaz took his first steps on the entry threshold leading into the one bedroom suite. The space also has a living room, a kitchen and a bath, along with two patios. One of the patios at the time was private enough to allow Desi, Jr. to practice his climbing skills on a tree; unfortunately, now gone and replaced by a Bird of

Paradise.

1194 Via Miraleste in the Movie Colony s a home in the Movie colony neighborhood which at some point in the 1990's began claiming that Lucy and Desi stayed there during their in between years in Palm Springs on the premise that the Arnazes sought to be close to the El Mirador hotel – it was just across the street – and yet wanted the privacy which an enclosed estate could provide. A good story. One that seems to fit the couple's intimacy concerns at this point in their lives. The home is strikingly beautiful in an old Palm Springs way. It's a single level Spanish Missionary charmer with lots of bougainvillea and wonderful poolside views of San Jacinto. The owner's agent stated openly that no documentation existed to verify Lucy and Desi's ever rented it. She further claimed that former Mayor Frank Bogert had told an old woman at the Historical Society, "the Arnazes had hosted parties here." Yet, when I called Lucy's and Desi's daughter, Lucie Arnaz, to verify these stories, a staff member told me, "They never lived there."

The Lost World Resort in Rancho Mirage was claimed to be an early effort of the Arnazes at private estate living in the desert. Author Ray Mungo, in his book: Palm Springs Babylon, St. Martin's Press, 1993, described it as, "...just a little walled kingdom, with bungalows for 75 couples, a dozen tennis courts, stables with horses, and ample room in the canyons for riding." He then goes on to tell how in 1982, after it had been sold by the Arnazes, this resort became one of the desert's first lavish gay resorts. I don't know. The difficulty is this resort was torn down prior to 2000 to make way for a new home development. The address doesn't even exist anymore, making research difficult. I do know that I personally delivered telegraphs and newspapers there in the 1980's, when it was an exclusive resort, and saw none of the openly sexual activities that Mungo claimed.

Blue Horizons Mobile Village is just down the street

from the Thunderbird Country Club and hosts a large collection of dated mobile homes which at the time might have seemed reasonably priced and trendy. Bing Crosby was the main force behind the development of this park and even though there were multiple celebrities investing with him, Lucy and Desi were not among them.

The only clear truth of where they stayed as a couple while in Palm Springs is printed in the 1954 Palm Springs book. We'll take a look at that in the beginning of the next chapter. Don't read ahead. We've got other life events still to cover in 1953 first. Still, where's there's a rumor there might be a small kernel of half-truths. Desi did come out to Palm Springs on his own at times and at other times he wandered around Palm Springs without Lucy even if she were in time. He was a skirt chaser and a gambler and Mayor Frank Bogert did retrieve Desi when Lucy asked. Desi had to stay somewhere. Some of these places that claim the famous couple stayed there, though they have no record to prove it, could be half right.

It had been two years since Lucie Arnaz had been born. I Love Lucy had a couple years of being America's number one show. And now, Lucy was pregnant again.

The night Desi, Jr., was born coincided with General Dwight Eisenhower's inauguration as President (1953-61) of the United States. Nearly a decade after the inauguration, Desi, Sr., was golfing with Desi, Jr., at the El Dorado Country Club in Indian Wells when they ran into the, by then, former President. Eisenhower spotted the two Arnazes and chided Desi, Jr., by saying, "Is this the little fellow who knocked me off the front pages?"

Desi, Sr., responded, "Yes sir, General. That's him."

Back at the clubhouse, Eisenhower bought Desi, Jr., a banana split.

1953 was also the year Lucille Ball was called a communist by the House un-American Activities Committee – though later the same year she was found innocent.

Though there were lots of highs in 1953, the low of beng alled a communist showed the Arnazes who their friends were too. One of them was Lou Costello, who was also a Palm Springs, Mesa neighborhood, resident. Costello was one of the first of the Hollywood crowd to return to their Chatsworth area home.

Otherwise, 1953 was a great year for Lucy and Desi and they returned back to Palm Springs in style. They signed a picture deal with MGM, the biggest ever at the time, for $250,000 to do the movie The *Long, Long Trailer.* One of the studio execs grumbled about the size of their paycheck, claiming Desi was holding a grudge against Ricardo Montalban's replacing him on earlier projects. Desi issued a gambler's challenge, offering that if the film didn't gross as much as Father of the Bride, a huge moneymaker for MGM in the U.S., Desi would give the studio back $25,000, but if it grossed more he and Lucy would be owed $50,000 more. It was written into the contract and a year and half later, the studio paid up.

The *Long, Long Trailer* was about a married couple, named Nicki and Tacy – definitely not Ricky and Lucy – and the Palm Springs scenes depicted a couple pulling a very long trailer over the top of treacherously steep Highway 74, which climbs out of Palm Desert into the coastal mountains toward Anza and San Diego. It was produced by Lucy's former admirer Pandro S. Berman, now living at 259 West Camino Alturas, in the Mesa neighborhood of Palm Springs. It also featured Marjorie Main, who had made her name as Ma Kettle in the *Ma & Pa Kettle* movies twenty years earlier. Main owned a home at 1280 South Calle Rolph in the Deepwell neighborhood of Palm Springs. And the show's Cinematographer was Robert Surtees, who would in 1967 purchase a Las Palmas neighborhood home at 1276 North Rose Avenue, Palm Springs.

Finally, in 1953, Desilu made a deal with one of Palm Springs most famous residents: Frank Sinatra. Sinatra was to star in a melodramatic show called *Downbeat*, about a struggling singer of a small combo band in New York. The singer would constantly be getting mixed up with women and mobsters and finding all kinds of trouble. Yet, he had a heart of gold and would somehow end up on top or at least out of the frying pan to continue another episode. At the time, Sinatra's career was in the dumps and the De-silu production looked very promising for a Sinatra revival. But before it could be made, Frank landed the lead role in From Here to Eternity which propelled him to new heights. To break his contract with Desilu, Sinatra offered to reim-burse production costs. Desi told him to, 'Fogeddaboutit it,' and generously let him out of the deal.

From the 1949 Palm Springs phone directory.

Desi during his opening run at the Chi Chi Club Starlite room in 1950 during what was called The Safari Waif Ball.

Desi singing a Latin song in Palm Springs in about 1950.
What do you think: Cuban Pete or Babalu?

Lucy and Desi blow out the candles on Desi's 34th birthday at a restaurant in the desert in 1951. The cake had miniature golfers and a horse stable on it.

Armstrong H W Mrs h Smoke Tree Ranch (box A) 47443
Arndt Simeon T (Anna) r Eagle Canyon Trlr Pk box 441 CC 48-4242
Arndt Victor M (Louise) pntr r Eagle Canyon Trlr Pk (bx 441CC) 48-4181
Arnell Louis r156 S Indian av
Arner Saml D (Desert Realty Co) h68-615 Broadway CC box 228 48-3251
Arnez Desi (Lucille B) actor h334 Hermosa pl
Arnholz Walter Mrs r1563 S Palm Canyon dr

Balkcom Geo W jr (Loraine) clk PO h68-791 B CC
Balkins A J h1478 N Palm Canyon dr
Ball Earnest W (Rachel E) (box 428)
Ball Lucille actress r334 Hermosa pl
Ball Rachel E Mrs slswn Bullock's (box 428)
Ball Richmond F Mrs h210 Camino Carmelita 44189
Ballaban Sadie maid r419 Valmonte Sur 42010

Both of these listings were in the
1954 Palm Springs phone directory

# 1954-1957
## Living in Palm Springs

BEFORE THEIR NEW Thunderbird Country Club home was completed, Lucy and Desi stayed at a temporary residence in Palm Springs. This is the one residence authentically verified as to the couple staying during their construction interlude: 334 Hermosa Place in the Las Palmas neighborhood of Palm Springs. It is bonafide because Lucy and Desi listed it as their home, along with their names in the 1954 Palm Springs phone book. At the time, the Spanish Hacienda style home was owned by Sam Goldwyn, President of Goldwyn Studios. The studio boss owned the home for a number of years, estimated from the 1940's to 1960 and used it as a rental or loaned it out to those actors and actresses he either wanted to woo into his stable of stars or as a reward for those he wanted to keep.

This makes sense too. It is a walled home, set back from the road, with a private backyard pool and a large front yard. Though reclusive, it's close to everything Palm Springs had to offer: The El Mirador, The Racquet Club, restaurants, The Chi Chi Club, down town, and more. It would have been the perfect hideaway for a famous couple with lots of friends and business acquaintances in the desert, who they would want to see from time to time. Yet, it would also have all the privacy and home like amenities a new mother would desire; especially when the mother had two babies to care for.

In 1954, *I Love Lucy* was in its fourth season. Desilu studios was now a major player in Hollywood and the Arnazes had climbed beyond the A-list of celebrity stardom. They were Hollywood royalty.

Season 4, Episode 26 of *I Love Lucy* was a parody of things to come. It was titled *I Love Lucy in Palm Springs*. In it, the Ricardos and the Mertzes had already moved to Hollywood, California as Ricky's entertainment career had taken off and he was being offered movie roles. Lucy, Ricky, Fred and Ethel were each becoming so annoyed with one another to the extent that instead of both couples going to Palm Springs for a weekend of relaxation, it was determined best if either the ladies or the men would go. A coin toss was the strategy used to settle it. Lucy flipped the coin, lost, and then claimed, "OK, two out of three." Tossed again. "OK, three out of five." Toss. "Four out of seven." Ricky grabbed the coin in midair and conceded the weekend to the ladies. While the girls were there, Ricky asked Rock Hudson to play a trick on them. Hudson pretended to nonchalantly stumble across the ladies poolside and told them a story of a man whose incessant whistling annoyed his wife to the point of their separation. Until the woman realized she loved the man none the less. Too late, the man had had an accident and died, and the bereft woman had lost her man. A real tear jerker. Lucy was crying by the time Ricky and Fred climbed from their voyeur hiding spot in the bushes. The entire episode was shot from the RKO/Desilu set, in Hollywood. The only real part of Palm Springs was the large photographic stills placed strategically outside the dummy windows which depicted a rainy weekend from the bungalow of the Smoke Tree Ranch area of South Palm Springs. In the end, the sun came out and a good laugh was had by all. Cue credits. Raise the ending theme song.

In real life, the Arnazes were determined to make

the desert lifestyle a centerpiece in their lives. Before building their permanent desert retreat at Thunderbird Country Club, Lucy and Desi rented a bungalow while it was still the Thunderbird Dude Ranch. But ever since 1951, when the ranch owners had decided to parcel out the land into lots along a newly built golf course, the couple had been anxious to become members, although they did not join the club through normal channels.

Lucy confided once to a close friend that Desi had won their lots in a card game with friends Buddy Rogers, Phil Harris and a few others; George Goodyear, George Firestone, she couldn't remember. Somebody ended up owing Desi $18,000 and as the stakes got higher than a fellow gambler could muster cash, the deed to two parcels of property was thrust onto the jackpot. Desi knew the lots were worth about $9000 each and felt they would rise in value over time. He allowed the bet to ride and deftly took the player's land with the flip of a card.

In 1954, Lucille Ball and Desi Arnaz finally completed construction on their new home in the Thunderbird Country Club at 40-241 Club View Drive, Rancho Mirage. It was designed by the famous Mid-Century architect Paul Williams and was situated between the 9th and 18th fairways of Thunderbird Golf Course. The home is a beige stone and glass 6 bedroom mid-century structure with 6 baths, a swimming pool, and landscaping which blends the outdoors with the indoors. It's designed to maximize the views by bending around panoramic greens and capturing the nearby soothing Desert Mountains which erupt stoically from the sand. It was her desert retreat, a place to relax and enjoy a bit of respite, while the rest of her life was spiraling onward and upward.

Even though they were seeking a private life away from Hollywood, they weren't the only celebrities who'd thought this way and Thunderbird Country Club found itself home to many unforgettable names. Their neighbors included: Bing Crosby, Dean Martin, Gordon MacRae, Clark Gable, the Firestones, Ginger Rogers, composer Jimmy Van Heusen, baseball great Ralph Kiner, Mary Pickford, Buddy Rogers, Phil Harris, Alice Faye, composer Hoagy Carmichael, and many more.

With friends and family such as these, it's no wonder that the Arnazes often accepted invitations to parties and special events. Frequently seen at the clubhouse and other establishments, such as The Racquet Club or Tamarisk Country Club, the two could always be counted on for a quick laugh and a rousing time of fun.

Early club members remarked that Lucy would come to the clubhouse after ladies golf day to visit members and within minutes would be up in front of the group doing some routine to gather attention; though others disclaim this, citing them a quieter couple in public. Yet, still others claim Lucy and Desi would show up at the club jam sessions. Desi would entertain, as would Bing or Dino or other members at the exclusive clubhouse.

Former Palm Springs Mayor Frank Bogert, who at the time was the General Manager of Thunderbird Country Club, remembered Lucy's relish for games. She devised one game where players would roll dice, but if you scored over a certain number you lost. At that point, the shooter would frequently yell, Sh*t!" Lucy, therefore, declared that to be the official name of the game and would simply say, "Let's play Sh*t!"

The desert was idyllic for the Arnazes, though there was a serpent in the garden. Lucy loved her home in Thunderbird. Yet, at times, Desi would have difficulty playing the golf course there. Jews, Blacks, Mexicans and apparently Cubans were not allowed to play the course regularly. Owning one of the first homes in the development was no guarantee of play for Desi. Hidden in a crop of Aloe Vera bushes was a membership sign that read: FOR THOSE WHO QUALIFY. The Management and HOA of Thunderbird

Country Club deny it to this day; but, at times, Desi would simply be told there were no available time slots to play golf even though he could see out his living room window that no one was on the fairway. It was very frustrating and due to this kind of prejudice Tamarisk Country Club was created nearby. Desi joined Tamarisk as a place to play when he ran into an unfriendly golf employee.

At the time, unknown to Lucy and Desi, there was a storm brewing and how they would weather it would affect them the rest of their lives. The only hint of it came late in 1954 when the owner of Motion Picture Center, from whom they were now renting substantial space for Desilu Pictures: a division of Desilu Studios, confided in Desi that he was considering selling the Los Angeles establishment on Cahuenga Avenue to an unknown buyer. Though Desi tried to pry the answer out of the owner, he politely refused. The owner had tried to sell it to Desi, but in those still early days of Desilu, Desi didn't have a mind to purchase the property.

What he did have a mind to do was enjoy his new-found desert home. Palm Springs was deep in its Golden Era with the Arnazes living in town. It was a magic time in Lucy and Desi's life when they got to enjoy a secluded paradise in a town full of friends. Outside activities were the norm during the day and invitations to dinner parties filled the nights. They were the happiest and healthiest they had ever been.

Unbeknownst to the happy couple though, the roller coaster ride they called their lives was in for a reality jolt. It was January, 1955, and <u>Confidential Magazine</u> was finally ready to take aim. The article detailed Desi's indiscretions; including his Palm Springs weekend while serving in the Army a decade earlier and the details of his rendezvous with the girl (Sally) rocked Lucy's world once again. It was a slap in the face to all they had created together. Though the article also revealed some more recent escapades of

Desi's he somehow convinced his red-headed bride that he was a changed man. Those deeds were in the past. He was now not only a devoted husband, he was the father of their children and for these reasons he would be truer than ever. A lesser woman might have ended it all right there. Lucy, however, chose to forgive, even if she couldn't completely forget.

Lucy and Desi had come a long way from the break out stars they had been not that many years before. They were now headliners, producers and very corporate. The tabloids were not kind – on that they could agree – and more and more often the couple sought a place where they could be a family in private. Over the years the desert would see the Arnaz children grow up among a group of Thunderbird celebrity peers and non-celebrity local children. The desert was the home where the Arnazes could be themselves and their children could just be kids. Frank Bogert's daughters Denni, Cindy and Donna would often play with Lucie and Desi, Jr., in the country club as would other local children.

Their *I Love Lucy* TV son, Keith Thibodeaux, was also brought out to their Thunderbird Country Club home. His credited name on the show had been changed to Richard Keith to protect his innocence and childhood. Keith became almost like a second son to Desi, who taught the boys how to swim, ride horses, handle boats and fish. Lucy and Desi hired Keith's father to work at Desilu and Lucy became Keith's acting coach; they often vacationed together in the desert.

Lucy was very proud of her talented children and she encouraged them to try a great many things. By the time Desi, Jr., was 11 he could play the drums, guitar, piano and trumpet. Little Lucie studied dancing, modern Jazz and piano at the same time. "Whenever they express an interest in anything, I come up with a teacher," said Lucy in a <u>Palm Springs Life</u> interview. "I think a lot of juvenile delinquency stems from parents who fail to teach their children the importance of accomplishment. When children, as well as adults, lack something to do, they look for other people with nothing to do – and then trouble starts."

The Arnazes found time for themselves too. One time, Lucille Ball, Lily Pons, Clifton Webb and comedian Danny Kaye, went to a house warming party in the new Mesa neighborhood, Palm Springs home of Miss Pons. "Twas a long night indeed," recalled photographer Gail Thompson of the 1955 party, in an excerpt from an interview in <u>Palm Springs Galaxy</u> magazine. "Most of her (Miss Pons) celebrity guests continued the celebration long after the conclusion of Lily's party, entertaining her and all present with their endless talents to make an unforgettable night."

The year 1955 also brought a new opportunity for Lucy and Desi. Thinking of the San Fernando Valley, Chatsworth Ranch remodeling and additions, Lucy considered Desi, at times, a frustrated architect and he got another channel from which to explore his dreams of design. The two bought 50 acres of land even further out from Palm Springs, in what would then be called the boonies of Indian Wells. It seemed that the desert was destined to become a golf haven, regardless of the prejudices of Thunderbird Country Club, and the Arnazes wanted their own piece of the proverbial pie. In 1956, what had once only been a sea of sand dunes opened as the Desi Arnaz Western Hills Hotel. Opening day was a fanfare event with chairman of the Board, Desi Arnaz, flipping tongs from a greenbelt barbecue. Celebrity friend William Frawley (Fred Mertz) attended along with other desert and Hollywood personalities who lined up to tee off on the new golf course while a gallery of spectators watched from lawn chairs.

Desi and a few other investors formed the Board of Directors with co-founders Paul Prom, Eddie Susalla, Lin Johnson, Earl Murphy, Milt Hicks, Bill Worthing and John

70

Courci. The club opened with a nine-hole golf course. A second nine holes opened under a tight deadline of April, 1957, due to a $25,000 bet Desi had with Frank Sinatra, who at the time was building his own new home in Tamarisk. The second set of holes opened on schedule and Desi collected his winnings, although it is said he lost more than he gained due to overtime charges from the contractors.

In a further demonstration of his business savvy, Desi outfitted the hotel with furniture and equipment from the same wholesalers who supplied Desilu and its productions. Desi took advantage of his celebrity persona and negotiated significant price breaks. Bigelow Carpets, a supplier, began running slick magazine and newspaper advertisements of the famous couple, seated cozily upon fresh plush weaves in their Thunderbird home at the same time the hotel received new flooring.

Lucy let the hotel be Desi's turf. She knew he wanted his own private showpiece in the desert and the hotel was it. He spent more than a million dollars on the forty-two room project. That amounted to more than $24,000 a room, not an inexpensive endeavor in those years. The main dining had a sunken bar featuring native Cuban drinks from Desi's personal recipes. Lucy claimed the architect tested the drinks first and then sunk in the bar area so people wouldn't have so far to fall. The Desi Arnaz Western Hills Hotel featured a large tile mosaic of Desi in the lobby and Desi bobble-head dolls were distributed to guests. And the house band was Desi's own orchestra he had toured with in previous years. Lucille's brother Fred Ball was hired as the hotel's assistant manager.

Desi liked imposing his personality on the project, had a hidden card room constructed on the second floor where high stakes poker was played. The room was named "The Snake Pit."

On one occasion at the hotel, Frank Sinatra thought

the Desilu production *The Untouchables* was a slur on Italians and the Mafia. Sinatra, who was out with his girlfriend Dorothy Provine and friend, song writer Jimmy Van Heusen, was overheard to say, "I'm going to kill that Cuban prick!" Desi nonchalantly replied "Hi ya, Dago." They faced off to fiercer words, but the two were separated by their respective body guards. Both men always had at least one protector on hand at all times. But, this time, Desi's were more numerous, since he was on his home ground at the hotel, and Desi laughed at the singers menacing words as he walked away. Sinatra's been heard to defend himself by claiming, "He didn't want to hurt a friend."

At the same time as the couple's desert life was blossoming, the Arnazes careers were on a roll. Their production companies of Desilu and Zanra had grown to epic proportions and they now had over a dozen shows on air or in production. *I Love Lucy* was the biggest hit show on television and Desi and Lucy were more in demand than ever before in their lives. Lucy was the fire-hot redhead who was comically on point whenever the camera was rolling and Desi was the production boss who knew every aspect of his business. But, behind the scenes, problems were brewing.

Much later in life, William Asher, who directed 110 of the 179 I Love Lucy episodes between 1952 and 1957, commented on the Arnazes, that '... professionally, you could never tell if there was trouble between Lucy and Desi.' Yet, when thinking back to his times playing golf with Desi and actor Phil Harris, Asher claimed, '... Desi wasn't very good. But we'd always stop along the fairway at Phil's house to pick up another bottle.'

The stress of being the head of such a big company was getting to Desi. Desilu had grown from a small group of less than ten people to a company that produced more than a dozen shows. Though the organization fostered a family atmosphere through picnics, bowling sprees, Disneyland trips and such, more and more often Desi was on the phone with New York at six in the morning and at the studio by 7:30am. He worked on a slew of shows all through the day including *I Love Lucy*, and then did not return home till after the dinner hour. His pace was frantic.

Lucy was busy all day too. *I Love Lucy* was an energy consuming show. But she was also taking care of Desi, Jr., and little Lucie too. Whether it was designed to compensate or not, their shows began to lengthen to an hour, but the run shortened to only five special shows a year. One of them was a bit reminiscent of their lives, detailing how their TV personas met. In the series, Lucy first met Ricky as a young secretary who went on a vacation to Havana with a co-worker girlfriend Ann Sothern. Rudy Vallee was on the same boat the two ladies took to Cuba and when the gals got to Havana they were met by two young men, Cesar Romero and Desi, who had a horse and buggy carriage taxi service.

This episode though, unfortunately, ended up running an hour and fifteen minutes. Yet, CBS had only designated a one hour time slot. To make the show fit the programming schedule, Desi had to call up the sponsor of the show following *I Love Lucy*, United States Steel, and ask them for some of their time. The U.S. Steel show was a dramatic anthology of various plays done live. Desi didn't think it was very good and told them so. What could have been a helpless blunder turned out to be a saving grace. Desi offered to come on at the end of *I Love Lucy,* as himself, not Ricky, and after thanking U.S. Steel for the extra fifteen minutes, tell the American people they should stay tuned for a great show by the Steel Company. Luckily, U.S. Steel, at the time, shared Desi's opinion of the lackluster show and were thankful for the boost in ratings their show would get following *I Love Lucy* that season. They were even more thankful for Desi's personal encouragement and promotion and it turned out to be one of U.S. Steels best seasons ever.

Still, work was hard, and eventually, Desi began seeing Doctor Marcus Rabwin for his stress. Dr. Rabwin's wife, Marcella, was a very good friend of David O. Selznick's personal executive assistant. Desi credits Selznick – who had produced *Gone With the Wind* in 1939 and at this time was seeing his latest and last production; *A Farewell to Arms,* starring Rock Hudson and Jennifer Jones – for teaching him a lot about the pre-production, writing, casting, planning, execution and post-production responsibilities of development. Dr. Rabwin listened to Desi's complaints of stress, long hours and drinking. In response, the doctor gave Desi a full check-up. The results were that Desi's colon was full of diverticulitis and continuous high pressure activities like long work hours and drinking would make it worse. Dr. Rabwin told Desi he had to cut back.

Impossible. The difficulty was neither Lucy nor Desi were ready to stop. Lucy could not fathom sitting around their Rancho Mirage home staring at Mount San Jacinto as she slipped into her golden years and watch the children grow up. She was still too young. Weekends, yes. Month after month, no.

They began going to Palm Springs or their Del Mar home for longer weekends as a compromise, but more and more often, Desi would bring Lucy, the kids and Desi's mother out to the desert and then he'd disappear. For him, it was go, go. go. Desi was off to golf, his hotel, his gambling. Even in his recreation he was a constant whirlwind of activity.

This postcard of Lucy and Desi's Thunderbird Country Club home was available at stores everywhere in Palm Springs until the early 1990s. Now it's a collector's item.

The Hotel del Tahquitz was the site of Desi's worst publicized cheating scandal. The actual indiscretion occured in 1945. Yet, <u>Confidential Magazine</u> chose not to run the article till 1955. The hotel was located on the corner of Baristo and Palm Canyon Drive, where the Modernism Museum now stands.

The November 1954 issue of Palm Springs Villager.

Lucy and Desi at lunch with friends in Palm Springs.

From left to right: Clifton Webb, Lucille Ball, Lily Pons, Danny Kaye, unknown person, Desi Arnaz and Ray Ryan (owner of the El Mirador hotel) at Lily Pons party in 1955.

Desi Arnaz and actor Bob Cummings.

Desi Arnaz out on the prowl at the Racquet Club's
Bamboo Lounge. Where's Lucy?

Celebrity entertainment was common in Palm Springs during this time. Notice the length of Lucy's script as compared to Desi's.

An artist's rendition of the soon to be completed
Desi Arnaz Western Hills Hotel and Country Club.

Desi's hotel even had helicopter limousine service
from the Palm Springs airport on the day of it's
Grand Opening on December 22nd, 1957.

Desi and friends, Mr. and Mrs. John Bromfield
have the first drink in the pool at the hotel.

The hotel pool under construction.

The completed pool area of the
Desi Arnaz Western Hills hotel.

This is an artist's conception of how the Desi Arnaz Country Club Lodge at Indian Wells will look when completed.

Mr. Arnaz will build, own and operate this beautiful lodge consisting of 42 air conditioned and heated units . . . all of them with service kitchens, bar and full bathrooms. Every unit will have its own patio with complete privacy yet each one will provide a full panoramic view of the golf course and foothills.

The lodge will have dining facilities for 200 and a magnificent sunken cocktail lounge in addition. All lodge guests will have club privileges during their stay and rates will be moderately scaled.

Swimming pool, of course . . . even a wading pool for the little ones.

DESI ARNAZ

# INDIAN WELLS GOLF and COUNTRY CLUB

P. O. Box 638    PALM SPRINGS, CALIFORNIA

This advertisement appeared in the October 1956 issue of Palm Springs Villager.

Lucy and Desi arriving to the Grand Opening of the
hotel in a helicopter from the short-lived Desilu
production of *Whirlybirds*.

The handsome couple during the evening
of the Desi Arnaz hotel Grand Opening.

Lucille Ball and former Palm Springs Mayor Frank Bogert.

Lucy and Desi standing in the lobby of their hotel.

Palm Springs Historical Society

Actor, owner of the Racquet Club, and Mayor of Palm Springs Charlie Farrell and Desi Arnaz laughing after finishing a game of Wisket.

Paul Pospesil Collection

The Desi Arnaz hotel in about 1960.

# 1957-1960
## The Studio Boss and the Comedienne

IN SEPTEMBER, 1957, the ante got upped. Desi received a phone call from one of David O. Selznick's former top people, Dan O'Shea. Dan was now representing General Tires share of RKO studios. Dan told Desi, "General Tires wants to sell." General Tires had originally bought RKO from Howard Hughes.

So, Desi called up Hughes for advice, telling him General Tires wanted to sell him Hughes former studio.

"What do they want for them?" Hughes asked.

"$6,500,000," Desi said.

"Grab it!" stated Hughes, explaining the value in the studio was in its extensive movie library.

In the next 24 hours Desi got a loan from Bank of America for $2mil for the down payment, negotiated General Tires down to $6.15mil and didn't tell Lucy about it till mid-performance of making a Shakespearean *Lucy-Desi* episode with guest star Tallulah Bankhead. Lucy came in to Desi's back stage office wearing a knight's suit of armor just as the phone rang. She heard Desi clinch the deal.

"What the hell was that all about?" Lucy asked.

"We just bought RKO Studios," Desi responded.

"We did what?"

"We bought RKO Studios," Desi repeated.

After the show, which was a blur to Desi and Lucy,

Eric G. Meeks

they stayed up all night talking about what he'd done. They were both flabbergasted and excited. Desi told her about the deal, his talks with Hughes, the negotiations and all the land, sets, and library film footage they'd bought. In the end, they both remembered a discussion they'd had a few years ago when they were scared Desilu was going to get gobbled up by a larger studio. At that time, they'd decided to get bigger to fend off a hostile takeover. Now, they weren't just bigger, they were the biggest! They now owned more soundstages than 20th Century Fox or MGM. They owned incredible sets, even the charred remains of Tara from *Gone With The Wind*. They owned dresses and costumes worn by the leading actresses and actors of the past fifty years. And more props, materials and decorations than they could imagine.

Desi became the studio's Chief Executive and top salesman. With the location of the studio's back lot, he took on shows that needed space and vistas: *Whirlybirds, Sheriff of Cochise, The Man Nobody Knows*, and more. Along with the new stages, new comedies and dramas were put *into production: This is Alice, The Ann Sothern Show, Guestward Ho,* assorted weekly comedy hours, and more. Some of these shows gave Lucy and Desi excellent cross-benefits. Desi was always a man who knew how to get the most out of any deal. For instance, because they were producing the show *Whirlybirds*, starring Kenneth Tobey and Craig Hill and they now had unfettered access to a corporate helicopter. It became fairly common practice for the busy couple to use the choppers as their own private limo service out to the desert during these years. They could even have one of the stunt pilots chauffeur them out to the hotel in Indian Wells, where they kept a car.

While Desi was gearing up for bigger and better business, Lucy, now in her late forties, was using all the extra workers and assistants to wind down her commitments so she could become more family-oriented and en-

91

joy her children, now 7, Lucie, and 5, Desi, Jr. *The Lucy-Desi Comedy Hour* became a once a month episode as part of the *Desilu Playhouse* series. She used a professional editor to finally compile all the thousands of hours of family home movies into a cohesive length of film and then went to work cleaning out closets. She did undertake one significant RKO project, creating a children's theatre workshop. With the help of $90,000 to rehab a building once used by Lela Rogers, Ginger Rogers mother, for the same purpose and after a little more than a month's worth of auditions, Lucy chose twenty-five kids to be a part of her troupe.

Desi and Lucy found their duties and responsibilities fulfilling at the new Desilu Studios and could now focus on the things they loved to do most. But real life never compares to the movies and a happy ending was not in store for the couple.

When they were out in Palm Springs, little did Lucy know that Desi was still leading a double life not just onstage, but in reality. He was spending some of his nights drinking in downtown Palm Springs at the Chi Chi Club Starlite Room and The Racquet Club's Bamboo Lounge, carousing with other male actors on the prowl for swooning female fans. These clubs were typical of the Hollywood era of Palm Springs, creating and ending many couples and marriages.

Lucy was in high demand locally, charities and other organizations were recognizing her worth as a publicity draw. Rancho Mirage was not an official city. It wouldn't be incorporated till 1973. But, the Chamber of Commerce was in full swing and they asked Lucille Ball to be the Honorary Mayor. She accepted and from 1956-1965 she hosted a number of events, ribbon cuttings and galas.

Desi on the other hand was earning a different sort of reputation.

According to Frank Bogert, "Desi was a bit of an enigma. A lot of people thought he was just a playboy. But, he knew every aspect of a show's production: the lighting, the script, the budget. He was running Desilu, a multi-million dollar company. By the end of the day Desi would be pooped. So he'd have a martini and that would lead to ten more and that would lead to girls. In chasing women, Desi started out with the prettiest ones and after several martinis ended up with the ugliest witches you ever saw."

"Desi was a good little guy, but a drunk," Bogert continued. "Whenever he would disappear, Lucy would send me looking for him. Whenever she sent someone from Desilu, Desi would fire that person, but he couldn't fire me."

"He was drinking quite a bit then," director Bill Asher recalled. "But he was a jolly drunk. Everybody paid court to him as a celebrity, but it wore off after a while."

Desi was down emotionally, but not out. He made one of his best business deals ever when he bought the rights to a book by Elliott Ness and started production of *The Untouchables*. Desi's first choice to play the FBI agent who bring down Al Capone was Van Heflin, a character actor with a long string of supporting and leading roles in action, western and detective dramas. But Heflin turned it down.

Desi's second choice to play Ness was Van Johnson, Desi's old stand-in from his first Broadway play *Too Many Girls*. With Johnson's All-American blonde-boy good looks, he was a natural to play the part of America's top cop. Johnson's career had been incredibly strong earlier in his life, but more recently was in a state of decline. He needed a good come-back role and was thrilled at the offer. But, Van's wife, Evie, was handling the contract negotiations and she blew it. She called Desi while he was in Palm Springs one Saturday night. She complained about Van being promised $10,000 to do the initial pilot episode, which was to be aired as a two-parter on Desilu's *Westinghouse Playhouse*. Evie got it in her head that since it was two segments, Johnson deserved two payments of $10,000 for a total of $20,000. The shooting was scheduled for Monday and Evie knew this. She tried to hold the show hostage unless Johnson got his double paycheck. Desi wouldn't have it. He fired Johnson on the spot. When Evie asked Desi what he was going to do come Monday, Desi replied, "That's my problem."

The answer to his quandary for a leading man was Robert Stack. Stack came from a very wealthy family and, after making the deal over a late night phone call from Desi, Stack started work the next day without a signed contract. *The Untouchables* raised Stack's career to new heights. Before the role of Ness, Stack had only been known as an up and comer; but, once he was the star of a prime-time TV show, Stack was a leading man who'd earned his credits legitimately. *The Untouchables* went on for 4 seasons with 118 episodes, plus the original two-parter. Stack, as Ness, first brought down Capone and then went on to enforce Prohibition in gangster riddled Chicago. Desi paid Stack well for his performances on the show. Stack made $750,000 and *The Untouchables* became the best dramatic show of its time.

Despite the success of Desilu, Lucy had had enough of Desi's late night escapades. In an effort to build the family one last time, she took Desi and the children on a trip to Europe to try. It didn't work. Desi was constantly bored and restless. He spent most of the trip with a drink in his hand and a phone glued to his ear talking to the studio, the racetrack, the hotel, or who knows who else. They returned from the trip not speaking to each other.

For the next year and half they continued life at the studio and home without much care or concern for each other. They went through the motions of a married couple; acted the roles of a Hollywood couple; an executive couple; a Palm Springs couple. But, their feelings were as dried up as the desert tundra.

Finally, on March 3rd, 1960, after nearly 20 years of marriage, Lucy filed for divorce for reasons of "Extreme Mental Cruelty."

Over time, denial would creep back into Lucy's head about Palm Springs. When she was asked if she and Little Lucie and Little Desi had visited the house often over the years, she shook her head, 'No'. To Lucy, the home had "bad memories" for the kids. It was in the living room of their Rancho Mirage home where Lucy and Desi had told the kids they were, "Splitting up."

Lucie, now nine, said, "You can split up, just don't get divorced." She and Desi, Jr. just didn't understand the severity of what was happening. As Hollywood children, they'd seen lots of their friends parents break-up, separate, or get divorced. But the kids just couldn't fathom it for themselves.

Lucy and Desi kept up the charade of being married for a few months more. But in reality, they were already living apart. Desi slept in another room. They went to work and performed and did business. Life wasn't good, business was great.

The final episode of the *Lucy-Desi Show* was an hour long with guest stars Ernie Kovacs and Eadie Adams, in which Lucy was trying to get Desi on Ernie's TV show. At the end, Desi and Lucy kissed as actors. At Lucy's prompting, Desi yelled, "Cut." Their marriage was over.

Lucy had filed for divorce and this time she meant to finish it.

Lucy and Desi enjoying their 12th anniversary
at Thunderbird Country Club in 1952.
Lucy is pregnant with Desi, Jr.

*Desi Arnaz'*
# INDIAN WELLS
*Hotel*
### AT INDIAN WELLS COUNTRY CLUB
#### Between Palm Springs and Indio

Full refrigerated air-conditioning. Studio rooms with bath, dressing room, TV, bar & patios. Exciting restaurant and Stage Bar. Swimming. Golf.

RESERVATIONS write P.O. Box TT, Palm Springs, or phone FIreside 6-6144.

### "DINING ROOM OPEN TO PUBLIC"

From the 1963 Palm Springs phone directory.

96

# 1960-1969
## Lucy After Desi

THE DIVORCE WAS fairly amicable. Everything financial was split down the middle, 50/50. Each received half of De-silu, then estimated at a value of 20 million dollars. Lucy got the mansion in Beverly Hills and the Rancho Mirage, Thunderbird home and Desi got the Del Mar estate. Lucy got two station wagons and a cemetery plot in Forest Lawn. Desi got a golf cart and the Tamarisk Country Club membership. The hotel would be sold when a suitable buyer could be found. Lucy got the kids during school times. Desi got them on the occasional weekend and holiday.

Lucille Ball wanted to get away from it all. She wanted to disappear to England or Switzerland and look out at rain, snow, mountains or some other depressing country vista to ease her state of mind. She packed up the kids, decided to sell both of her homes in Beverly Hills and Palm Springs - which thankfully, she never did – and instead, ended up making a movie with one of Palm Springs most famous personalities, Bob Hope. It was called *The Facts of Life* and was about two people who weren't fond of each other in the least. But when their spouses couldn't join them on an annual group vacation to Acapulco, Ball and Hope end up going it alone and have an affair. During the filming of a boat scene, Lucy fell hard while stepping off the dock. She injured her leg and gave herself a concussion severe enough to put her in Cedars of Lebanon hospital. Desi rushed to her to make sure she was alright. When he found she was not permanently injured he sent Bob Hope a telegram joking, "I played straight man to her for nine years and never pushed her. Why couldn't you control yourself?" The movie won Ball a Golden Globe for Best Actress and it was nominated for four Academy Awards.

Desi and Bob were great friends, despite the barb. In 1960, Desi played in Bob Hope's very first golf tournament, which would eventually become the Bob Hope Classic. The tournament grew out of the Thunderbird Invitational and was won the year before by Arnold Palmer. Desi played in the budding golf tournament for years as did many other celebrities.

"He (Desi) was very enthusiastic about the tournament," recalled Ernie Dunlevie, tournament sponsor and developer of Bermuda Dunes from a Palm Springs Life interview, "and he gave us a hand whenever and wherever needed." The event was eventually played at Desi's golf course in Indian Wells well into the 1970's. Lucy was a regular attendee of the Bob Hope Classic Ball.

After making her film with Bob, Lucy travelled as far as New York, where instead of hiding from life she chose to take her career on a new path by starring in the show *Wildcat*, a western musical where her character, Wildcat Jackson, was broke but determined to strike oil.

She decided to go her own way and Desi could run Desilu Studios. It didn't quite work out that way though. How could the gray skies and cement structures of New York compare to the bright horizons of the west? She mistakenly thought the kids would love New York and be able to entertain themselves on the small outdoor patio her high-rise quarters provided. She quickly found out they preferred their friends back in California.

*Wildcat* received mediocre reviews from the critics.

'Worshipful fans,' as the critics wrote, packed the audience night after night. Lucy broke fingers, sprained ankles and lost 19 pounds while performing. She loved being on Broadway, but the kids preferred their friends in California. A week or so after the show started, on December 20th, 1960, a good friend took her to a pizza dinner to introduce her to a guy. Gary Morton. Lucy's first reaction to the invitation was no. She claimed to need rest for the show, but her girlfriend persisted and Lucy finally went.

She was really in no mood to meet a new man. She was pushy and stand-offish. When she demanded Gary light her cigarette, he told her, "Light it yourself."

He was just what she needed; someone to put her in her place and not kowtow to her like she was a Hollywood big shot. They got along tremendously, though nearly fifteen years separated them in age – she was nearly fifty. He was 35 – Gary looked older than his years. It helped. So did the fact that he was sober and could be a steadying force in Lucy's life. Furthermore, he was a travelling comic who'd already headlined and played opening acts for the likes of Sinatra, Dean Martin and Sammy Davis, Jr. He knew his way around a stage and didn't hide from the spotlight. What was even more perfect was that he'd never seen a single episode of *I Love Lucy,* because during its run he was performing around the country doing his own shows. In early 1961, Gary asked, "Would you be my girl?" Lucy never dated anyone else after that.

With the children's acceptance of Gary and the blessing of her priest and mentor, Dr. Norman Vincent Peale, who performed the services, Lucille Ball and Gary Morton became married on November 19, 1961 at the Marble Collegiate Church in New York.

For five months, Lucy did little except be a mother to her kids and a wife to Gary. Then Desi talked Lucy into playing in another series: *The Lucy Show,* about two single women raising their children on their own. Vivian Vance

was brought in as her sidekick again. The show had its mo-
ments, but the most difficult ones were from the sidelines.
Having both Gary and Desi just off camera proved to be
nerve wracking. After some discussions, Desi disclosed
that he was ready to retire anyways and in November,
1962, Lucy bought him out of his Desilu shares to the tune
of nearly $3 million. The Board of Directors encouraged her
to accept the President's seat. She accepted and found
herself the head of a major motion picture studio, producing hits like: *Ben Casey, The Andy Griffith Show, My Three
Sons, My Favorite Martian*, and *The Danny Thomas Show.*

On March 2, 1963, Desi married another red-head:
Edith Mack Hirsch. She shared his love of horses and fish-
ing. Lucy thought the two were a good match. The two
newlyweds flew to Las Vegas to be married at The Sands
hotel and eventually ended up purchasing their own home
in Thunderbird Country Club at 71475 Mashie Drive, Rancho Mirage, not far from Gary and Lucy.

That December, Lucy wanted to take Gary and the
kids on a traditional winter holiday. After calling on her old
friend Bette Davis, she chose a place in Francois, Connecticut and crammed everyone into a small chalet, eating
out every meal, and freezing in the north eastern winter. At
some point during the trip, Gary remarked, "And to think
we have that wonderful place in Palm Springs."

Of all the homes that Lucy owned, the Thunderbird
Country Club home, near Palm Springs, was Gary's favorite. When given the choice, he would bring Lucy and the
kids out to the desert every time. Often, Gary's mother,
Rose, or his sister, Helen, would come out and join them
in the desert. Lucy was generous in this way. On at least
one occasion Lucy did mention to Rose that she would give
Gary anything he wanted, but if she ever caught him even
looking at another woman, she'd kill him.

Early on in their relationship, Lucy, Gary and Gary's
mother  Rose went to a party at  Frank Sinatra's house in

Rancho Mirage. Sinatra was at one of his high points in his career. This would've been about the time *Sergeants 3* was in the theatres and not too long after *Oceans 11* was made. It was the era of The Rat Pack successes and Dean Martin and Sammy Davis, Jr. and the rest of the gang would have been riding high on their popularity. At the party Rose sat on the sofa talking with Sammy, Peter Lawford and Frank, along with Gary who kept pointing out the other celebrities for his mother. When Pat Kennedy Lawford was introduced, Rose spoke up saying she knew Pat's brother, President Kennedy, very well.

"You know my brother?" Pat replied.

"He gave a speech in my neighborhood," Rose whispered confidently.

Another thing Lucy did in Palm Springs was to star as the 1964 Queen of the Desert Circus Parade. The Desert Circus was an annual week-long event where celebrities and local dignitaries hosted many special events and fundraisers with a decidedly western flair. Cowboy hats and spangles adorned handsome men and pretty ladies all over town. Notables were rounded up and thrown in front of a mock judge who declared donations, disguised as penalties and fines, in front of invited media to raise funds for charity. The week would culminate in a grand parade down Palm Canyon Drive with its Queen or King riding in the back of a fancy convertible waving to the thousands of adoring fans.

Desi ran into a bit of trouble during the mid-1960s at Thunderbird Country Club when he was sued by an older couple for allegedly punching out a man in front of his wife. As the story goes, it was New Year's Eve and Desi and Edie were at the club's front office seeking a room to rent for the night. Desi had been drinking and made rude comments to the man's wife. When the man attempted to vocally defend her, it was claimed Desi hit the gentleman.

The famous lawyer, Melvin Belli, represented the

the couple in court. They claimed that Arnaz was both "mean and nasty" and "That he was a hell of a nice guy."

Desi's lawyer warned him that if Belli got him, Desi, on the stand he would attempt to make him lose his cool and explode. Desi calmly replied, "Don't worry.. When I'm on the stand I'm Ricky Ricardo." Plus, Desi had a star witness who had seen the whole affair from the parking lot, through the big windows of the front office.

As if on cue, Belli called Desi to the stand and did his best to shake him up. He asked if Desi had called the man's wife a !@#$%.

Desi replied in a very even-tempered tone, "I'm a Cuban gentleman. I would never call a woman that. You, (indicating Belli) I would call that."

The audience and jury roared with laughter.

Now came the star witness.

A large nosed old man rose from the audience and came forward to be sworn in by the bailiff, asking the man to first state his name.

"James Francis Durante," the man replied. After his defensive testimony was given, the jury deliberated for only 17 minutes before delivering a verdict of "Not Guilty."

In 1967, Lucy sold Desilu Studios to Gulf+Western, who renamed it Paramount Television. The company is now called CBS Television Productions. The top shows Desilu was producing at the time of the sale were *Mission Impossible, Mannix, The Lucy Show,* and *Star Trek.*

In 1968, Lucy started her own production company called: Lucille Ball Productions. That same year she produced and starred in her own show titled: *Here's Lucy,* which ran until 1974.

Warner Borthers Pictures Publicity Photo

In 1962, Lucy starred opposite long-time desert friend Bob Hope in the Technicolor comedy *Critics Choice*.

Lucille Ball as the1964
Queen of the Desert Circus Parade

Lucy across the street from what is now See's Candies, downtown Palm Springs.

Desi Arnaz and friend, Eddie Susalla, playing golf together at Thunderbird Country Club in the 1960's.
Susalla was also an investor and board member
in the Desi Arnaz hotel in Indian Wells.

# 1970-1989
## Till Death Do Us Part

IN 1970, DESI sold his Thunderbird home to actress Kaye Ballard, who co-starred opposite Eve Arden, in the 1970's Desilu hit, *The Mothers In-Law*. Prior to her purchasing the home, Ballard had been a frequent guest there and borrowed the home when it wasn't in use. Ballard called Desi, 'A true romantic,' claiming he often left the refrigerator stocked with champagne and caviar. She bought the home fully furnished. During her desert breaks, Ballard also visited her friend Lucille Ball and remembers spending hours just sitting, chatting and playing games.

In 1971, the Chamber of Commerce asked Lucille Ball to be Honorary Mayor of Rancho Mirage again. The city was really becoming a desirable place to do business. A number of new country clubs had opened up, as had a plethora of businesses and Eisenhower hospital was already up and running with its first building. Lucy couldn't say no and she served again from 1971 to 1973 when Rancho Mirage officially became a city.

There was only one time that Lucy and Gary's marriage hit a genuine "rough spot." That was when Gary took it upon himself to redecorate the Thunderbird home without Lucy's permission. He did it as a birthday surprise for her; redoing the living room, dining room, kitchen and master bedroom. He had new drapes, carpets and wallpaper installed, bought new furniture, and Lucy hated it. She threw a fit. They argued. They ranted back and forth at each other over his changes. In the end, Gary conceded and Lucy won. They didn't talk for weeks, but eventually, they reconciled after Lucy redecorated the home the way she liked.

During her show business slow down years, Lucy's love of games kept her entertained. She'd loved word games since she was a child, but more recently she'd discovered a new game, Backgammon. Backgammon was her tour de force and she was known to play against Joe Burns, a desert resident who cared for celebrity homes. He'd met her one Christmas as he was passing out Poinsettias to Thunderbird neighbors and had knocked on Lucy's door. Joe recalled their meeting in a Palm Springs Life interview.

"What do you want?" She snapped at him with decades steeled sharpness.

"Merry Christmas," said Burns. "I want to give you this plant and be your friend."

She melted and they became friends. After that, they would usually get together for a game or two at Lucy's house, though not always. Once, she called him up and asked, "Joe, can I come over?"

"As if I could say no," recalled Burns. "Who says no to Lucille Ball?"

Another time he was invited over to Lucy's house and Gary Morton answered the door. Morton said, "Come on in. Lucy is still putting on her make-up. She doesn't do that for me!"

One habit Lucy had that Burns remembered was crouching over while she walked and smoked throughout her home as a means to fool the smoke detectors. "Lucy smoked like a fiend," Burns stated. "When going down a hallway with her cigarette, she walked bent over like Groucho Marx, so she wouldn't set them (smoke detectors) off as she had several times."

She also loved Wheel of Fortune and Jeopardy! She would spend most evenings watching her favorite shows and smoking Phillip-Morris cigarettes. Phillip-Morris had been the original sponsor of the I Love Lucy show. In the daytimes, she watched Password and $20,000 Pyramid while listening to Bobby Darin and Dean Martin records.

Because of Lucy's deep friendship with Betty White and her husband, Alan Ludden, Lucy guest starred on Password a few times. During taping of the show, she was a nervous wreck. She was afraid she wouldn't be good enough for her partner. Of course, that is a joke in itself. Lucy had always had a love of games. She was good at them. But, because of her nerves she stuttered her way through the entire show.

In 1977, Lucy's mother, Dede, died. Her full name was Desiree Evelyn Hunt and she was 85 at the time of her death. She'd been Lucy's number one fan her entire life and had shown up for the taping of more episodes of *I Love Lucy, The Lucy Show,* and *Here's Lucy* than anyone else. Her distinctive gasps of, "Uh-oh," can be heard on many of the laugh tracks. At the time of Dede's death Lucy was 66.

As the years passed on, Lucy changed. It's hard to say when, but perhaps it was because of all the times of having to listen to Desi "Splain" himself or perhaps it was from their divorce; it could have been when Lucy had to take over Desilu Studios and do the one thing she really hated doing – firing people. Or perhaps it was simply a life-time of being overly adored for her acting and not being herself most of the time. An actor's life, especially a successful actor, can shift Heaven and Earth and make a person behave in the most unacceptable of ways. Whatever the reason, Lucy had hardened over the years. Long gone was the aspiring young actress with stars in her eyes. She was one of the most famous actresses in America. Over time, she became very reclusive and only let a select circle of people into her life.

When writing this book, from time to time, I came across someone who'd worked for Lucille Ball: a gardener, a maid, a driver, a nurse; or the son or daughter of an employee. Many said something about how hard or mean or critical Lucy had been of them. Once, an adult, who as a child had been allowed to play with Desi, Jr., and Little Lucie, shared that he had broken one of Lucy's kids toys. Lucy had fumed and thrown the playmate out of the home. Nearly all who talked to me refused to go on record and asked me not to include their stories.

Life can be cruel and life can be kind, and so could Lucy. All in all, I find these stories no surprise. As much as we loved Lucy, love had not always been kind to her. Even adoring fans can get a bit 'in your face' with their adoration, when uninvited, yet still wanting 'just a moment' please.

Still, at other times, she was called a mentor and a great lady during the interviews of former long-time employees and people who knew her as a struggling young actress. Often I was told a tale of their being given a leg-up when Lucy became a star and how Lucy rewarded those who knew her back when from her own struggling days. These people knew her and loved her.

Her marriage to Gary had turned into one of the best things in her life. He was exactly what he appeared to be from the moment they first met, a stabilizing force. She was that and more to him too. She gave him instant credibility and the ability to explore the things in life he had dreamed of. Once Gary married Lucy, he could get onto evening talk shows, she bought him suits and cars and he developed a distinctive increase in style. Though they owned Bentley's and Rolls Royce's and Mercedes, their best known car was the 1986 Chrysler Lebaron convertible with wood side paneling that they kept in Palm Springs. Lucy hated how the car talked to you whenever a seat belt was unbuckled, a door was left open, a tail light was out, etc. She called it the Chrylser Mother-in-Law, because it was constantly nagging her.

Another time, Gary had a large television set delivered to their Thunderbird Ranch home. While he was out, Lucy found the large console TV with its huge wooden encasement, reminiscent of a coffin. She hated it. The delivery men were very interested in showing Lucy the multitude functions of the remote control which raised and lowered the actual television out of the console. It had VCR capabilities and even picture in picture display. She let them go on and on without disclosing the fact that she was completely lost. A technologically backwards lady, Lucy wasn't very interested in this next generation of electronics. Even her phones were still rotary dial in the new age of push button. Instead of letting the delivery man know her lack of interest, she simply let them drone on till they were done, then set the remote aside.

Morton was also able to direct and produce movies. He did direct one, though to no apparent success. However, as a producer, Gary Morton had a hit that further cemented another new star to the forefront of the American psyche when he selected Tom Cruise to play a young Pennsylvania steel town football star in the movie *All the Right Moves*.

As the seventies became the eighties, Lucy and Gary fell into a routine. Beverly Hills was their full-time home, Palm Springs their winter retreat. Christmas was in Beverly Hills. New Years was in the Thunderbird home. They were often invited to Frank Sinatra's and the gala New Year's Eve events at Bob Hope's, whom she deeply loved and admired as the consummate professional. As far as can be discerned, Lucy and Gary seldom accepted and instead chose to spend time with closer friends. More and more often though, they simply kept to themselves.

Lucy even tried playing a round of golf once with fellow actress, friend, and Palm Springs resident Dinah Shore. But, Lucy was lousy at it and spent most of the day in the sand traps or the rough. The other golfers kept yelling for her and Dinah to 'hurry up.' It wracked her nerves and she never played again.

Lucy also tried horseback riding. Unfortunately, her injured leg from *Wildcat*, though healed, was never the same and she found being in the saddle too uncomfortable.

Backgammon was her thing and she really enjoyed it. She kept boards everywhere and played often. She enjoyed playing for the constant challenge of the game. It challenged her mind, her playing skills and her luck. No matter how well she strategized there was always the roll of the dice to make the game exciting. She liked playing against different people. In Los Angeles and New York, she had backgammon clubs she went to. In Palm Springs, she went to Melvyn's Ingleside Inn to find new partners. On Tuesdays and Thursdays the Inn hosted a backgammon night and Lucy would arrive with a driver or a friend and play against comers in the crowd. This went on till the crowds grew too big and it seemed more of a show than a fun night out.

In 1986, at the age of 75, Lucy made and starred in another TV series called *Life with Lucy*, produced by Aaron Spelling. Spelling had once, as a young actor, played a part in an *I Love Lucy* episode as a country bumpkin opposite Tennessee Ernie Ford. *Life with Lucy* was the first real flop of her life. 14 episodes were supposed to be made. But, when Spelling was informed by ABC, in November, that the show was due to be cancelled because of poor ratings – it was 73rd of 79 shows being made that year. Spelling called Gary Morton, who worked with Spelling, and told him not to tell Lucy till after the season was finished. 13 episodes were made, but only eight were aired. The show was never syndicated and was only rerun once on a Nickelodeon Lucille Ball marathon in 1999. Lucy never made another movie or TV show and rarely did an interview ever again.

112

A few months later, on December 2, 1986, Desi Arnaz died of Lung cancer in the Del Mar home which he had received in the divorce decree 27 years earlier. He was 70 years old. Director William Asher shared a story with Palm Springs Life that best illustrates the essence of the union between the famous comedienne and her hot-blooded Cuban lover.

"She visited him in Del Mar a week before he died," Asher revealed. "By this time, his ailments included emphysema and the colostomy he'd had for a couple of years. Desi was out of it, disoriented. When it came time for Lucy to leave, Desi said, 'Where are you going?'"

"I'm going home," Lucy responded.

"You are home," Desi said. So, Lucy stayed a while longer.

"Lucy told me this at Desi's funeral in Del Mar," said Asher. "They had a love that was lasting in spite of their differences."

Kaye Ballard, who knew and was a friend of both said, "She was in love with him until the end. And he was in love with her."

Danny Thomas delivered the eulogy at the funeral. Slowly, life moved on for Lucy.

On Thanksgiving 1988; Gary, Lucy, some of Gary's family and friends of Lucy's came out to Palm Springs for the long weekend.

The first thing Lucy did was give her guests a tour of the home, starting with the master bathroom. The room had all the necessary bathroom features along with a full-blown office, complete with desk, rotary phones (Lucy never did upgrade to the digital touch tones), and a wall full of family photographs, most of them her grandkids. She was very proud of her bathroom office.

Lucy then led her group into the backyard where they saw a breathtaking view of the fairway, a small bridge spanning a cleft in the ground separating the course from her home. She had a modest pool and a comfortable patio fringed with seasonal flowers. Lucy led the group past these features in a comical follow-the-leader fashion, walking like Charlie Chaplin, waddling with an imaginary cane twirl, doing a jump and spin, and then she paused and pointed at the ground. Stretching beneath the group's feet was a shallow chasm of split earth. Lucy declared this to be the spot where she had "...the scariest experience of her life." She said she'd been in the desert with Dr. Norman Vincent Peale and his wife when an earthquake struck the area. Everything was shaking. The quake had nearly knocked her over while she was coming back towards the house from a swim, as the ground pulled apart. It just opened up. She pointed to the exact spot where the fissure now lay open like a wound of jagged rocks. She'd feared that she would fall in and then it would reclose, crushing her. The sound was something she'd never heard before. Few have. It made her even more afraid. Then, luckily, it had all stopped.

Lucy never explained exactly which earthquake she was referring to. There had been two major earthquakes in the Coachella Valley during her ownership of the Thunderbird home. On 15th October 1979 a 6.5 earthquake struck the Imperial Valley, centered about 30 miles from Lucy's home. The other was a 6.0 on 8th July 1986, centered in North Palm Springs only 10 miles away as the crow flies. The latter is the most likely to have caused the rupture Lucy described. Throughout the Palm Springs area, it left several fissures scattered, split roads, and caused a fairly substantial amount of damage to homes and businesses.

The weekend also included an unpleasant encounter over Lucy's lemonade which created a growing unease from those around her as they did not wish to challenge her. Lucy was known to not accept criticism well. Apparently, Lucy had made some lemonade which her friends knew was going to be surprisingly tart. When they attempted to tell her that it was too sour, Lucy refused to allow them to sweeten the mix. As they tried to make light of the situation and cajole her into accepting their criticism, a friend made a mocking reference to "poisoning."

Lucy yelled for some plastic glasses, and after some argument over who should perform the taste test, thrust it at her friend and demanded he see for himself how good it was.

What could he do? He drank and collapsed on the floor grabbing his throat and bulging his eyes in a melodramatic display of death.

To prove him wrong, she swiped the glass away and tried it herself. Her lips immediately pursed from the overly sour lemonade. When she regained control of her facial muscles, she parsed, "It needs more Sweet 'n' Low."

Over all, it was a fun filled weekend of Backgammon and sunshine. On day two of the weekend, the fun hit a snag when the scorekeeping showed that the players owed Gary's sister, Helen Maurer, $112,000. One player had been keeping score. But due to the excessive losses of the other players, Lucy derided him and tried to find a mathematical error. When she couldn't correct the figures easily, it was the players turn to chide her, claiming "How could you run a studio and not be able to add?"

"I hired somebody who could," she yelled back.

Laughter chorused and they broke for a lunch of left-over turkey.

That weekend, Lucy also divulged that her husband, Gary Morton was having the same difficulties which Desi used to have over not being allowed to play Thunderbird Country Club's golf course. Apparently Jews were still not allowed and Gary, like Desi, played his rounds at nearby Tamarisk Country He couldn't even eat at the clubhouse, despite being a homeowner there. The group was astounded that in the late 1980's a practice like this could still be enforced. When one of the guests encouraged Lucy to push Gary to sue the country club, Lucy said, 'Gary would never do that, He was too much of a gentleman.'

Lucy loved to drive. But Gary would often refuse to let her. One time, while in Palm Springs, Lucy begged to take the Chrysler to the beauty salon and Gary conceded. Turning right out of Thunderbird, Lucy noticed the traffic was unusually heavy for a mid-week day. The weather was great and the town must have been filled with high season visitors. Lucy made it to the corner of Bob Hope Drive and Highway 111 when the Chrysler conked out at a traffic light. Lucy's understanding of auto mechanics was extremely limited and she simply sat there turning the key over again and again in the ignition, to no avail. Cars began honking at her, making her frustration levels rise. When a police cruiser finally showed up, one officer directed traffic around her car while a young police woman stepped alongside the driver's window and convinced Lucy to sit on the curb as traffic passed. Lucy was nearly in tears. The female officer chatted with her as they waited for the tow truck. They talked about how the desert had grown over the years and about the current Mayor of Palm Springs, Sonny Bono. Lucy complained she would never make it to the beauty salon and the officer offered to take her in the squad car. Upon arrival, Lucy took off her glasses and gave the young lady a smile and a thank you. "You're Lucy," the officer stammered. Lucy thought the officer had known who she was all along, but the officer had simply been as nice as she might have to any other desert resident.

On December 31st, New Years Eve, 1989, Lucy and Gary stayed in Palm Springs, surrounded by Gary's family and a few friends. Backgammon was the entertainment, of course. Lucy had suffered a stroke six months earlier and was speaking with a slight slur because of her crooked mouth. A Richard Burton biography had come out recently, maligning Lucy as an overbearing actress and she was in

**116**

a state of depression over the whole thing. The inevitable result? Increased refusals to go out. Behind the mask of her stroke injured face, laid her injured pride. She'd always admired Burton and his wife, Elizabeth Taylor. So much so, that Lucy had even asked them to be on a *Here's Lucy* episode.

As the midnight hour approached, Lucy's spirits ran lower. Her friends and family tried a new card game Dean Martin had taught Lucy called Pig. Midnight finally came. They all put on funny hats bought from Woolworth's and toasted the New Year with a bottle of Cristal, a Christmas gift from Carol Burnett.

Lucille Ball-Arnaz-Morton and her husband Gary lived a good portion of their time, very reclusively, in the Club View Drive home in Thunderbird Country Club, remaining desert residents until their ends. Gary played golf while Lucy enjoyed the clubhouse in relative obscurity amongst the aging celebrity crowd. Sometimes they dressed down and went out together on jaunts to the supermarket in Gary's Chrysler Lebaron. Lucy had a favorite restaurant nearby, Dominicks, a well-known secret amongst the locals for great Italian food that was only a mile or so from their home.

During her final years, Lucy was crowned one more time, cementing her position as "The Queen of Comedy." Ironically, her last aired performance, on 30 March 1989, was a 61st Annual Oscars comedy special entitled *The Living Legends* honoring Lucille Ball and long-time Palm Springs resident Bob Hope.

That same year, she spent Easter Week in Palm Springs and confided to her daughter Lucie and gathered family that she had reached an agreement with Putnam to begin work on her autobiography. But Lucy never completed it. Lucie would finish and publish the biography seven years later for her mom, posthumously.

About a month later, on 26 April 1989, the girl born

as Lucille Desiree Ball, known to millions simply as Lucy, died of complications from a heart attack at Sedars-Sinai Hospital in Los Angeles. She was 77. In a final attempt to save her life, she had her aorta and aortic valve replaced with donor organs from a 27 year old man. All too late. Her curtain was falling and would not rise again. She was survived by her husband, Gary, who died of lung cancer in 1999, at the age of 77 in Palm Springs, CA. Lucy's brother, Fred Ball, lived on till 2007. He died at the age of 91 in Arizona.

Palm Springs still loves Lucille Ball and in 1995, as a memorial to her long commitment to Palm Springs, the city had a bronze statue of her placed at the center of downtown, in 1995. It can be found at the corner of Tahquitz Canyon Drive and Palm Canyon Drive, where all her friends and fans can remember Lucy.

In the Fall of 2012, Lucie Arnaz and her husband, Lawrence Luckinbill, bought a home in South Palm Springs. Then they bought another.

Lucy playing Backgammon at the Ingleside Inn
in the late 1970's.

Lucille Ball and Ingleside Inn owner Melvyn Haber.

This slightly larger than life sized statue of Lucille Ball sits at the corner of Palm Canyon Drive and Tahquitz Canyon Drive, downtown Palm Springs.

# *Palm Springs Thru the Decades*

EVEN IN TODAY'S Palm Springs, it's easy to run into people you know at the Supermarket, the streetfairs, in the restaurants, time and time again. And this in a city of nearly 50,000. If you include the entire desert area of Greater Palm Springs, the ten cities that make up the Coachella Valley: Palm Springs, Cathedral City, Rancho Mirage, Palm Desert, Bermuda Dunes, Indian Wells, Desert Hot Springs, Thousand Palms, La Quinta and Indio, there's some 450,000 year round residents, and you still run into people who can call you by your fist name.

Imagine how easy it was to do in the 1930s when the population of Palm Springs was only a cowboy town of 500 people and the entire desert area maybe reached 3,000. By the 1940s, the population of Palm Springs had grown to about 3,500 due to the growing tourism economy. Still, that's a very small town. You'd come out to the desert and check into one of the few hotels. If you didn't mind spending a bit, you'd go right for the El Mirador, the Desert Inn, or maybe the Racquet Club. Any of these would be littered with other celebs or Hollywood movers and shakers. If you were more interested in exclusivity, you might go for one of the boutique hotels, like the Casa Cody, or the Ingleside Inn. Still, if budget was the concern, there was the Hotel del Tahquitz or the Lone Pine hotel. From October to April, anywhere you stay you were almost certain to have a good time, run into friends at various points in their careers, and enjoy sunshine, freedom from the press, and have a distinct possibility of making a connection with someone who back at the studio could only be referred to as "Sir" or "Mam." Your first day would probably be no more than a quick dip in the pool and a casual drink as you settled in for the afternoon.

When evening came – early as it always does with the sun setting behind Mount San Jacinto – the Palm Springs phone book listed only 31 restaurants in its business section. The downtown strip was maybe three blocks long. On it, fine dining was limited to the Chi Chi Club, the Doll House, Don the Beachcomber, or The Dunes. And the Hollywood crowd would be oh so recognizable. They'd stand out. See that amazingly beautiful young lady over there, the one with the suave-looking mature gentleman?. Wasn't she in that movie? You know the one. And that quirky guy over at the other table, the one with the glasses and the not so combed hair, he wrote a fantastic screenplay. And, I'd swear that man in the corner with the bass voice trying not to be seen – but who could help not noticing him? He wears the weight of the world on his shoulders easily enough and spends money like he carries the wealth of nations – he's a producer or a studio boss.

Now, if you were at the Chi Chi Club there'd be live first class entertainment. People like Liberace or Nat King Cole or Lena Horne might be on stage. If you didn't have exact plans, you might just go hopping to a favorite bar or two seeing who you could run into. Or, if you preferred a bit of danger and excitement, you might just go out to Cathedral City on Date Palm Drive and brave Al Wertheimer's Dunes Casino. It wasn't exactly legal, but no one was ever busted there. For some reason the police just turn a blind eye to the shenanigans; perhaps, because it was so far off the beaten track from the rest of the town and on a dirt road and all. Whatever you do, wherever you go, people are polite, gracious and welcoming. The stars shine bright both in the town and in the sky. A light jacket is needed – just enough to be stylish. And by the end of the night, you return safely to your hotel.

In the morning, you and your friend: girl friend, fiancée, or the man of the month? You both decide to have some outdoor activity. The sun shines bright and comfortably warm and it's time to do the things you can't do back in crowded Los Angeles. Tennis sound nice. There are available courts at any of the nicer hotels and if you play at the Racquet Club or the El Mirador, there's the added bonus of having a nice brunch while there. After lunch, you decide to go horseback riding. But, you forgot riding clothes. So, it's off to Marge Riley's Western Wear in the new Plaza shopping center downtown. While there, you go ahead and take a window shopping stroll of the shops and see such places as Charles Walters Men's Wear or Andrea Leeds Jewelry, always fun. The horses are most likely out at Smoketree stables on the south end of town, although you could just as easily go to the Deepwell stables or the Casa Cody, which was owned by a real relative of Wild West showman Buffalo Bill Cody. If you really wanted to escape the city you might go all the way out to Thunderbird Dude Ranch in Rancho Mirage. But, if you ride from Palm Springs there's always the Indian Canyons to explore and the creeks make the desert flora and fauna seem much livelier. Plus, if you go from Smoketree, Cary Grant, that hunky-hunk, and Fess Parker both keep their horses there. You might just run into somebody.

A few hours after setting out, you've had loads of fun. But, your butt is sore and it's time to think about a warm hot tub or perhaps a massage. Back to the hotel you go and once refreshed, it's time to consider the evening activities again. Now, which restaurant was our other choice last night?

And so it goes in Palm Springs. A town small enough that by your second or third trip, even if you aren't an A-list star of the film industry everybody knows your

your name.

During the 1950's, the year round population has grown to about 8,000. But, things have changed only slightly in the desert. Namely, there are a few new developments and a couple of golf courses have opened up. It seems chasing that little round ball might one day be a popular sport.

Some of Lucy's friends have purchased homes in the desert, allowing them to visit more frequently. People are talking about which sand dunes have the best chance of increasing in value. Still, the neighborhoods closest to downtown, like Las Palmas, or the Movie Colony – named for the crowd at the El Mirador – offer the easiest access to your favorite haunts. But then there's that newer district growing further South called the Mesa, and even down valley has started its destination transformation since Thunderbird Dude Ranch has become Thunderbird Country Club. Dinner talk is more about architects, designers, and builders. These things happen when success comes to your circle of friends.

New hotels have emerged, like The Ocotillo, Biltmore and Club Trinidad. But the old standby of the Racquet Club is happening too. The El Mirador became a hospice retreat for the returning servicemen of the European and Pacific fronts. Those guys gave so much; they deserve their time in the desert too. After all, many of them trained out here either in the upper desert, or out by Indio, or at that dirt field airport out on the edge of town, the one at the end of Tahquitz.

The favorite restaurants are still in business, though it's harder to get a table. You actually have to call first. There are some new ones. But, they're more for the growing crowd of seasonal tourists. Still, it's just a few extra places to run into new friends or to mix with polite fans. It's so nice that the in crowd from Hollywood has really sunk their teeth into Palm Springs. The locals have really taken a shine to showing their guests a good time in town. Some of the locals have really benefited too. God bless them. Why, even that one really nice hotel manager, Frank Bogert, has been elected Mayor a couple of times; as had the film star and Racquet Club owner Charlie Farrell. It's getting so it's hard to tell the film stars from the city founders.

By the 1960's, things were really heating up in Palm Springs, which now had a population of 13,500. The neighborhoods were a who's who of Hollywood elite, business leaders, and political professionals. Fundraisers to establish hospitals host charity events that look like the Oscars. Even just going down to your personal clubhouse can lead to an introduction with one of the Rat Pack, a Marx brother, or a chance encounter with any number of stars of the big and little screens. Bob Hope started a golf tournament that's really turning heads and helping promote that game. President Eisenhower is even being claimed to consider playing in it.

Some of the builders of the custom homes have taken to developing track housing with a nifty style. They like a lot of simple designs. It's very modern. Open garages, lots of glass walls to take in the views and high ceilings dominate the new homes. They're very affordable. Some go for as little as $29,000. It's allowing a lot more people to enjoy the desert in a more permanent way. Just the other day I saw a cinematographer and a set designer drive away from one of the sales centers. I hear that one gentleman from The Dorsey band bought a home for himself and his wife. They're such a nice couple. But, boy howdy, is this going to change the exclusivity of Palm Springs.

Then, in 1963, Troy Donahue, Connie Francis, Robert Conrad and that new actress Stefanie Powers introduced the world to the desert in such a big way with that hit movie *Palm Springs Weekend* about a bunch of college aged kids coming out during their Springs Break. Now, everyone wants to enjoy the sunshine and good times here. A whole new generation of people discover Palm Springs and while at first they only come for the week or two around Easter when their colleges our out of session, eventually they graduate and start looking for jobs. Some settle in Palm Springs and the surrounding cities. The entire desert has a name these days. It's called the Coachella Valley. And, before the end of 1965, Palm Desert opens its own campus of upper education. It's called College of the Desert.

In the 1970's, middle-America comes to the desert in a big way. Palm Springs residents now total over 20,000. Those housing tracks the developers have constructed fill up with families. Cities begin incorporating to govern the burgeoning middle class: Rancho Mirage and Palm Desert, both in 1973. The celebrities have aged a bit from their heydays in the desert and they don't walk the main drags as much as they used to. But still they can be found. By the 1980's down valley golf developments are erupting from the desert. La Quinta and Cathedral City both officially becomes cities. Owning a home or condo on a golf course is affordable for just about everyone and anyone who's anyone owns a home behind a guarded gate. Exclusivity comes at a price these days and the world has to be kept at bay. The phone book has hundreds of listings for restaurants across the valley. But, Lucy's favorite hang-outs get closer to home and more selective. That's OK. She's aged too and doesn't want to travel as far. Many of her friends are now gone to that great studio lot in the sky and her final curtain is drawing to a close. The years were great in the desert. She came and played, fell in love, escaped the hustle and bustle of Hollywood, saw friends, raised a family, got divorced, loved again, grew old and then it was time to say goodbye. She lived a life and we're all just thankful some of it was in our own backyard.

# *Friends, Family and Co-Workers*

## Film and TV Credits
## Cross-Referenced with
## Palm Springs Home Owners

## 720 East Paseo El Mirador
# EDDIE CANTOR

Stage and film star, Eddie Cantor, owned this Palm Springs Movie Colony neighborhood 3 bed, 3 bath 1941 home with 1,618sf, from 1944-1964. Cantor was wiped out financially in the stock market crash of 1929. But, his upbeat songs are credited with lifting America's spirits.

Cantor starred in Lucille Ball's first feature length film, Roman Scandals. where Ball, was a Goldwyn Girl and was cast as an uncredited extra.

## 2981 North Davis Way
## JACKIE COOPER

One of the few child actors from the Our Gang comedies who made the transition into adult roles, Cooper bought this 3 bedroom, 2 bathroom home in 1960. **It has 1632sf on a 10,019sf lot and is located in the** Racquet Club Estates neighborhood.

When Cooper did The Bowery with Lucille Ball, he was only 11 years old and already an established veteran of the silver screen. He'd been in 24 films over his young life at this point, including being nominated for a BEst Actor Academy Award for his lead role in Skippy (1931). In World War II, Cooper joined the Navy and later in life became a Captain in the Navy Reserves, using his Hollywood fame to help enlistment drives.

## 1055 North Rose Avenue
# JACKIE COOPER

In 1962, only 2 years after buying the Davis Way home, Copper upgraded to the Las Palmas neighborhood with this 4 bedroom, 4 bath, 2,799sf home.

At the time, he was married to his third wife, Barbara Rae Kraus, whom he had three children with: Russell (1956), Julie (1957) and Cristina (1959). He was a regular of TV during these years and his most current projects were Hennesey, The Dick Powell Theatre (another PS resident), The United States Steel Hour, and The Great Adventure. During the 1970's, Cooper would return to the big screen for his role as newspaper editor Perry White in the Superman films starring Christopher Reeve.

## 1129 East Tamarisk Road
# WILLIAM GOETZ

In 1955, Louis B. Mayer's son-in-law, Goetz, then the Head of Production at 20th Century Fox and Universal, leased this 5 bedroom, 6 bath, 4,074sf home, built in 1938. In his younger days, he produced films with several cameos of Lucille Ball's films,

including: *Broadway Through a Keyhole* (1933), *Blood Money* (1933) *Moulin Rouge* (1934), and *The Affairs of Cellini* (1934). It's likely that at the time of Lucy's arrival in Hollywood many of the up and coming stars and starlets would overhear the celebrity elite talking about their good times out in Palm Springs, creating backroom gossip and not so hidden desires of those wanting to be whisked away to the desert paradise.

## 1062 East Buena Vista Drive
# RAOUL WALSH

Built in 1937 with 3 bed-
rooms and 5 baths in 3,098sf
of interior space on a
10,019sf lot. It was home to
actor/director Raoul Walsh,
who made *Thief of Baghdad*
(1940), *High Sierra* (1941),
*The Naked and the Dead*
(1948), and more. But before
he made any of those big
hits, Walsh directed a little
known actress named Lucille

Ball performing an uncredited role in *The Bowery* (1933).

## 346 East Tamarisk Road
## JOSEPH SCHENCK

President of United Artists and Producer of Lucille Ball's first film, *The Bowery*, Schenck built
this home in 1935 after divorcing actress
Norma Talmadge. That same year, he part-
nered with Darryl Zanuck to found 20th Century Pictures and two years later he merged it
with William Fox's studio. The new company
was called 20th Century Fox. In 1943, Schenck was found guilty of tax
evasion coupled with a mob payola scandal to quiet unions.

## DARRYL F. ZANUCK

Quit Warner Studios to partner
with Schenck and created the
movie studio system. Zanuck con-
veniently won this house in a
poker game from Schenck while
Schenck was trying to evade an
IRS audit. The home is 7,247sf
with 10 bedrooms and 9 bathrooms. Zanuck died in Palm
Springs of a heart attack in 1979.

## 2905 North Puerta Del Sol
# CHARLES BUTTERWORTH

This journalist and actor who spoke the famous line, "Why don't you get out of those wet clothes and into a dry martini," worked with Lucille Ball on her ninth film *Bulldog Drummond Strikes Back* (1934). Butterworth owned this 7 bedroom, 7 bath, 4,743sf home, built in 1935, on a 41,382sf lot till his death in 1946.

La Quinta, CA
# FRANK CAPRA

Capra produced *Broadway Bill,* casting Lucille Ball in an uncredited part. Shortly after, he made *Lost Horizon,* shooting some of the Shangri-La scenes in Palm Springs Tahquitz Canyon. He supposedly wrote the script at the La Quinta hotel and, in 1961, purchased an A. Quincy Jones designed home on the 10th fairway. He died in La Quinta of a heart attack in 1991.

*Lost Horizon*
A
Frank Capra Production
COPYRIGHT MCMXXXVII
BY COLUMBIA PICTURES CORP OF CALIF. LTD.
HARRY COHN, PRESIDENT

## 334 West Hermosa Place
# SAM GOLDWYN

The movie mogul owned this home till 1960. It was built in 1926 with 4,574sf of space, 4 bedrooms and 5 baths, a pool and sits on a 18,731sf lot. He used it as a reward for the stars wanted to keep in his stable and as a lure for the ones he sought steal away from other studios. Lucille Ball and Desi Arnaz listed

home in the 1954 Palm Springs phone directory as their residence while they were having their Thunderbird Country Club hom e built. Goldwyn produced several films of the struggling young Ball's, including: *Roman Scandals* (1933), *Nana* (1934), & *Kid Millions* (1934).

## Smoketree Ranch
# GEORGE MURPHY

George Murphy was a dancer, actor, and a politician. He began his Hollywood career in 1930 and after appearing in many big musicals, he retired from acting in 1952 and switched to politics where he was Chairman of the Republican State Central Committee and then became a U.S. Senator. He was also a Vice-President of Desilu studios.

# 2294 North Starr Road
# LEO TOVER

Cinematographer of Lucille Ball's 1934 uncredited show, *Murder of the Vanities* went on to do *The Great Gatsby, The Day the Earth Stood Still* and more than 100 others. Tover lived in this 1,200sf, 3 bedroom, 2 bath home till he died in 1964. It was built in 1959 on a 10,890sf lot.

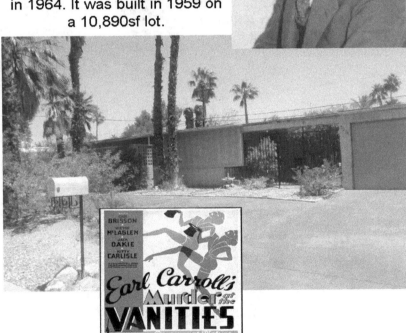

## 1075 South Manzanita Avenue
# LORETTA YOUNG

Young was already on her 53rd film when she and Lucy worked on *Bulldog Drummond* together in 1934. She didn't buy her Palm Springs house till 1993, only one year before she played her 107th role. The home is a 1964, 3 bedroom, 4 bath, with 3,510sf. She began acting in 1917, at the age of four.

## 259 West Camino Alturas
# PANDRO S. BERMAN

This producer and early admirer of Lucy's, cast her in numerous roles: *Roberta* (1935), *I Dream Too Much* (1935), *Follow the Fleet* (1936), *Room Service* (1938), helping establish her

as "Queen of the B's." In later years, he produced Lucy and Desi's movie *The Long, Long Trailer* (1954), shot on Highway 74 in Palm Desert. Berman lived in the West Camino Alturas home in 1951. It was built in 1945 with 5 bedrooms and 5 baths, 2,576sf on a 13,504 sf lot.

141

## 133 West San Carlos Road
## SAMUEL BRISKIN

This co-founder of Liberty Films would eventually produce such big hits as *It's a Wonderful Life* (1947). But, some of his more moderate budget projects included Lucy's films *Broadway Bill* (1934) and *Carnival*

(1935). Briskin's Palm Springs home was built in 1947 with 3 bedrooms, 3 baths, and 1,720sf on a 7,841sf lot.

## 1145 East San Juan
## BETTY GRABLE

In 1935, Grable acted in two films where Lucy had uncredited roles. In *Old Man Rhythm*, Grable had a supporting actress role and in the short *A Night at the Biltmore Bowl* Grable had the lead. In 1958, Grable was a guest star on Season one, episode four of the *Lucy-Desi Comedy Hour* in which she helped Lucy win a racehorse for Little Ricky. This Palm Springs Movie Colony West home was rumored to be the famed actress's during her second marriage to Trumpetist Harry James, 1943-1965. Facts are uncertain as to the authenticity of this claim. The 3 bedroom, 2 bath home was built in 1934 with 2,010sf of interior space on an 8,276sf lot with a pool and a guest house.

# 2965 North Puerta Del Sol
# PAUL LUKAS

Leading man actor built this 3,335sf home in 1935 for $4,750. That was the same year Lucille Ball played a minor role in *The Three Musketeers* with him. It has 3 bedrooms, 4 baths, a pool and sits on a 37,462sf lot.

## 282 West Camino Carmelita
# JOHNNY MERCER

Lyricist/composer lived in this 5 bedroom, 3 bath Palm Springs home with his dancer/wife, Ginger Meehan, and their kids. He first worked with Lucille Ball in *Old Man Rhythm* (1935) as a supporting actor, then in *That's Right - You're*

*Wrong* (1939), as a supporting actor. Though these were acting roles, Mercer was primarily a lyricist. To date, his award winning music has been used in over 600 shows, hundreds of times posthumously: *LA Confidential, Ocean's Eleven, Minority Report, Marilyn*. He was also the co-composer for *Meet McGraw* (1957-1959), a Desilu Studio Production. Johnny Mercer died in 1976.

## 701 North Patencio Road
# MARY PICKFORD & BUDDY ROGERS

Buddy Rogers played the role in *Old Man Rhythm* (1935) in which Lucille Ball was cast in an uncredited part. Shown here is the former home of Rogers and his wife, Mary Pickford. It has 4 bedrooms, 5 baths and 3,486sf on a 22,216sf lot, with a pool.

## 13 Cahuilla Hills Drive
# LILY PONS

International opera star Lily Pons owned this home with her conductor/husband Andre Kostelanetz in 1956. It was built in 1955, has 4 bedrooms and 5 baths with 3,529sf on a 39,204sf lot. Twenty years earlier, Pons had the leading role in *I Love Too Much* (1935) that portrayed a budding

Lucille Ball in an uncredited role. Pons worked again with Ball in *That Girl From Paris* (1936), where Pons again starred, but this time Lucy got a credited role as Clair. Lucy and Lily stayed in touch over the years and when Pons had her housewarming party at this Mesa neighborhood home, Lucy was one of the many stars in attendance.

## 999 North Patencio Road
# EDWARD G. ROBINSON

This actor, best known for playing gangster roles, starred in *The Whole Town's Talking* (1935), where he played the dual roles of a meekly accountant and the bank robbing killer who he actually resembles. It was Lucy's 18th film and she was still playing an uncredited bank employee. But, she was working. Robinson's Palm Springs home was designed by architect A. Quincy Jones and built in1959. It has 3 bedrooms and 6 baths, with 6,307sf on a 44,431sf lot with a pool.

## 375 West Via Lola
# ANDREA LEEDS

Leeds had a supporting actress role in *Stage Door* (1937) in which Lucille Ball portrayed Judy Canfield. Two years later, Leeds married Robert Howard, whose businessman father owned the racehorse Seabiscuit. But, the son did

not have the financial skills of his father and he went through millions in a short period of time. Leeds had jewelry stores at the El Mirador hotel and downtown Palm Springs. In 1951, Howard and Leeds hired architect O. E. L. Graves to remodel the Colonial House hotel, which was then renamed the Howard Manor. In 1954, they built their Las Palmas neighborhood 4 bedroom, 5 bath, 3,777sf home on a 17,860sf lot at 375 West Via Lola.

## 523 West Camino Sur
# ADOLPHE MENJOU

Menjou played attorney Billy Flynn in *Roxie Hart*, which inspred the play and movie *Chicago*. Menjou lived here in 1946. The Spanish colonial home was built in 1936 with 2,639sf and 4 bedrooms, 5 baths, on a 15,682sf lot.

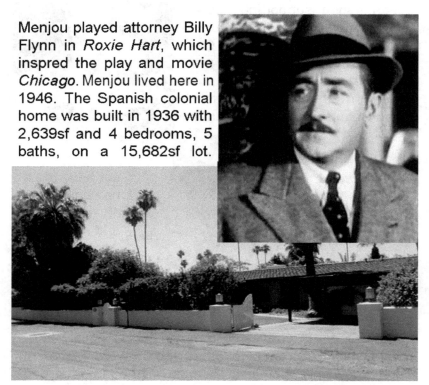

in 1937, he played a supporting role in *Stage Door,* about a boarding house full of aspiring actresses, in which Lucille Ball played the part of Judith.

## 457 West Hermosa Place
# ANN MILLER

The tap dancing star of stage and screen acted in multiple films alongside Lucille Ball: *Stage Door* (1937), *Having Wonderful Time* (1938), *Room Service* (1938) and once with Desi Arnaz in *Too Many Girls* (1940). Miller bought this Las Palmas neighborhood home from Donald F. Duncan, owner of Duncan toys, who made the Yo-Yo a household item.

## 1022 East Mesquite Ave.
# DICK LANE

Paramount Studios actor, Lane, worked with Lucille Ball when they were both younger, in such films as *Go Chase Yourself* (1938) and *A Girl, A guy and a Gob* (1941). But, :Lane's big break came in the 1950s when he was asked to be the announcer for Wrestling at the

Los Angeles Olympic Auditorium and then for the Roller Derby team (The Fabulous) Thunderbirds. He retired to Palm Springs in 1974 when he bought this 2,081sf home which was built in 1951 and has 3 bedrooms, 3 bathrooms and a pool sunk into a 10,890sf lot.

## 71111 La Paz Road, Rancho Mirage
# HARPO MARX

Harpo, the silent clown of the Marx Brothers, and though most of his brothers had a Palm Springs connection, Harpo's is the strongest to both the desert and to Lucille Ball. She plays opposite the brothers in the movie *Room Service* (1938). But, it was Harpo who came on the *I Love Lucy* show in 1955 and did the mirror routine with Lucy as Harpo in a hilarious bit. There are also several rumors about Harpo in the desert: 1) He helped form the Tamarisk Country Club when Thunderbird CC wouldn't let Jews, Blacks or Mexicans play. 2) That he would sometimes play golf in the nude. And, 3) He had his ashes buried in one of the sand traps there. Two other Marx Brothers have Palm Springs stories also; Groucho bought a home for his third wife, Eden Hartford, in central Palm Springs and Zeppo's ex-wife, Barbara, married Frank Sinatra.

# 1115 East Deepwell Road
# & 813 South Beverly Drive
# HARRIET PARSONS

Producer of celebrity documentaries, which included Lucille Ball in *Screen Snapshots, Series 18, Number 1* (1938) and *Meet the Stars #6: Stars at Play* (1941). Parsons bought the Deepwell Road, 2 bedroom, 2 bath home when it was new in 1955 and then purchased the South Beverly Drive 3 bedroom, 2 bathroom, 1,858sf home below when it was new in 1958.

## 1139 East Mesquite Avenue
# GINNY SIMMS

This singer and actress played in her first role when Lucy was on her 44th: *That's Right-You're Wrong* (1939). Simms bought her first Palm Springs home in 1956, when it was brand new. It had 2,227sf, 3 bedroom and 2 baths atop a 12,197sf lot with a pool. At the time of the purchase, she was a single woman, between marriages. In 1993, she received a star on Palm Canyon's Walk of Fame and on April 4, 1994, she died in her other Palm Springs home at 1578 Murray Canyon Drive. She's buried at Palm Springs Memorial Cemetery in Cathedral City.

## 985 La Jolla Road
# DONALD WOODS

The actor, not the B-picture movie producer of the same name, lived in this South Palm Springs Twin Palms neighborhood 1957 home in 1966. It has 3 bedrooms and 2 baths with 1,600sf and a 10,890sf lot. He worked with Lucille Ball on the 1939 film *Beauty for the Asking*, her fortieth film.

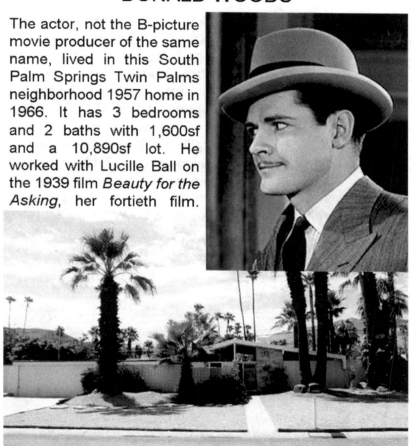

## 1575 North Via Norte
# EDGAR BERGEN

Ventriloquist, Bergen, shown here with his #1 dummy, Charlie McCarthy, played the lead in *Look Who's Laughing* (1940) opposite Lucille Ball, who played his assistant, Julie Patterson. Bergen owned this Las Palmas neighborhood Palm Springs home from 1947-1951.

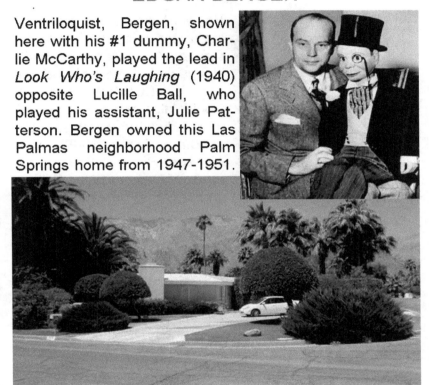

## 235 West El Portal
# LOUIS HAYWARD

Hayward played the supporting actor role of Jimmie in
*Dance Girl Dance* (1940)
alongside Ball, who played the
part of Bubbles. Hayward
would later achieve fame for
more adventurous roles, such
as *Black Arrow* (1948), *The
Masked Pirate* (1949), *For-
tunes of Captain Blood* (1950)
and more. From 1969-1985,

the swashbuckling South African actor
and his wife, model June Blanchard, lived
in this 2 bedroom, 4 bath 1,912sf Mesa
neighborhood home, built in 1951.

158

899 North Avenida De Las Palmas
878 Avenida Palos Verdes
# HAROLD LLOYD

Lloyd was one of the first people in Hollywood to recognize Lucille Ball's capacity for comedy when he produced the film *A Girl, A Guy and a Gob* (1941). In coming years, he and a few others would help her develop those comedic skills when Lucy and Desi were ready to depart the studios and begin their own:

Desilu. This 7,006sf, 5 bedroom, 6 bath home was built by silent screen star Lloyd in 1935 on a 43,996sf lot with a pool. The actor owned it till his death in 1971. The rear entrance address is 878 Avenida Palos Verdes.

720 East Cottonwood Road
# HENRY TRAVERS

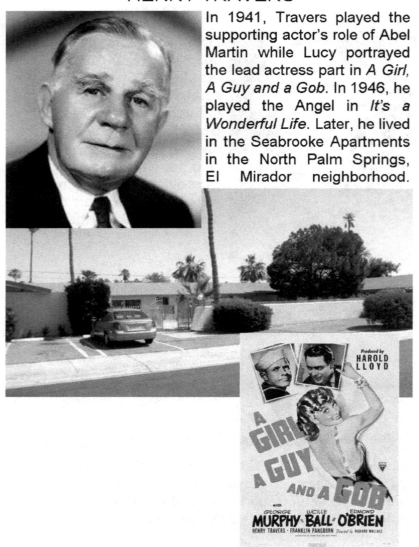

In 1941, Travers played the supporting actor's role of Abel Martin while Lucy portrayed the lead actress part in *A Girl, A Guy and a Gob*. In 1946, he played the Angel in *It's a Wonderful Life*. Later, he lived in the Seabrooke Apartments in the North Palm Springs, El Mirador neighborhood.

## 975 South Paseo Dorotea
# PAUL SAWTELL

Sawtell, who later in life was the Music Supervisor for such hits as *77 Sunset Strip, Maverick and Hawaii Five-0*, originally worked for RKO studio writing music for many B-movies, including the score for *Valley of the Sun* (1942) which cast Lucille Ball in the lead role of Christine Larson.

Composer lived here for two years. it's a 3 bedroom, 2 bath, 1949 home with 1,614sf of space on a 12,197sf lot across the street from Demuth Park.

## 675 West Camino Sur
# TONY MARTIN & CYD CHARISSE

In 1935, Tony Martin starred in the short film *Foolish Hearts*, which cast Lucille Ball in an uncredited role and Cyd Charisse had un-credited roles in T*housands Cheer* (1943) and *Ziegfeld Follies* (1945) which both had significant roles for Lucy. Nightclub entertainer

and actor-husband, Martin, and ballet dancing actress-wife, Charisse, moved into this home when it was brand new in 1958 and raised two sons here. It has 4 bedrooms, 3 baths, 2,534sf, a pool and a 12,632sf lot.

## 1011 East El Alameda
# BING CROSBY

Bing Crosby and his Orchestra played in *Thousands Cheer* (1943), which included Lucille Ball as herself. Bing resided here with his first wife, Dixie Lee, and their sons in 1936. The home has 3 bedrooms, 3 bath and was built two years

earlier in 1934 with 3,237sf of living space on a 13,058sf lot. Crosby owned several properties in the desert, including a home in Ironwood Country Club, a home in Thunderbird Country Club, and a ranch in the Silver Spur neighborhood of Palm Desert.

## 823 North Topaz Circle
## TOMMY DORSEY

Bandleader Dorsey acted in *DuBarry was a Lady* (1943), along with his Orchestra, which starred Lucille Ball **opposite** Red Skelton. Brother to big band leader Jimmy Dorsey, Tommy was a band leader and trumpeter

in his own right. Tommy's widow, Janie, bought this 4 bedroom, 3 bath, 1961 home in 1967 with 2,238sf on a 10,019sf lot.

### 465 West Merito Place
# LENA HORNE

Civil Rights Activist and black actress bought this 3 bed, 4 bath home with a pool originally under an assumed name in the late 1950's. It was built in 1956 with 3,869sf on a 24,829sf lot. She worked with Lucy in Thousands Cheer (1943) and Ziegfeld Follies (1946).

## 1516 South Manzanita
# WLADZIU VALENTINO LIBERACE

Famed pianist's first Palm Springs home, which he bought new in 1957. The 3 bed, 4 bath, 3,083sf home was built in 1956 on a 10,890sf lot with a pool. Liberace performed in several projects alongside Lucy, including: *Best Foot Forward* (1943), where he played an uncredited pianist and, years

later, he guest starred on *Here's Lucy* (1968-1973), where he played himself. Liberace loved Palm Springs and owned four homes there, plus bought another one for his mother. Liberace's second PS home was his guest house, located in the Sunmor neighborhood. The home was built in 1958 with 4 bedrooms and 4 baths, and 2,550sf.

## More Palm Springs Homes of
# LIBERACE

231 Lyn Circle, Sumor Neighborhood

His third PS house was built in 1952 in the Las Palmas neighborhood and had a piano shaped black mailbox, 3 bedrooms, 6 baths, with 3,101sf on a 14,375 lot.

1441 North Kaweah Road, Las Palmas Neighborhood

Liberace owned his main home on Belardo Road from 1967-1987. He renamed the home "Casa De Liberace." After remodel after remodel over the years it is now 5 bedroom, 7 bath home with 6,094sf, a fountain and a pool.

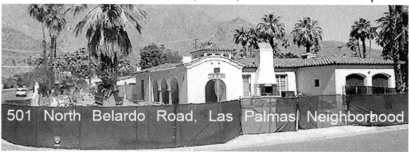

501 North Belardo Road, Las Palmas Neighborhood

## Camino Mirasol
# DONNA REED

Actress who starred in *It's a Wonderful Life* (1946), *From Here to Eternity* (1953), and her own TV variety show, *The Donna Reed Show* (1958-66) owned this home until her divorce in 1971. It was built in 1934 with 7 bedrooms and 6 baths on a 31,799sf lot. In 1943, Reed acted in the movie *Thousands Cheer* as did Lucille Ball.

## 37801 Thompson Road
# RED SKELTON

This Vaudeville clown, who made it big in radio and then on TV, first worked with Lucy in *Having Wonderful Time* (1938), then co-starred with her in *DuBarry was a Lady* (1943). He also worked with her in *Fuller Brush Girl* in 1950 and was on *The Lucy-Desi Comedy Hour* in 1959, when the Arnazes went to

Alaska and Lucy becomes panicked while flying with Red in a small bush airplane. Lucy and Red shared a mutual respect for each other's clown-like style of comedy their entire life. Skelton owned this Tamarisk Country Club 3 bedroom, 5 bath 3,528sf home on a 19,076sf lot, in Rancho Mirage, till he died in 1997.

## 1276 North Rose Avenue
# ROBERT SURTEES

In 1967, veteran camera-man, who won three Oscars, lived in this 4 bedroom, 3 bath, 2,560sf 1962 home on a 13,068sf lot. He was the Cinematographer for two of Lucille Ball's films: *Meet the People* (1944) and *The Long, Long Trailer* (1953).

## 1810 South Mesa Drive
# LOU COSTELLO

Comedic actor, who was one half of the comedy duo Abbott and Costello, lived here in this 2 bedroom, 2 bath, 2,250sf home in 1948. It was built in 1926 on a 10,454sf lot. He and Lucille Ball performed together in *Abbott and Costello in Hollywood* (1945).

660 Compadre Road
# A. ARNOLD GILLESPIE

Special effects pioneer who specialized in miniatures and received 12 Oscar nominations lived here in 1964. The home was built in 1958 and has 3 bedrooms and 3 baths comprised of 1,682sf on a 10,454sf lot. He worked on many of Lucille Balls projects over the years: *Without Love* (1945),

*Abbott and Costello in Hollywood* (1945). *Ziegfeld Follies* (1946), *Easy to Wed* (1946), and in 1953 Desilu Studios hired Gillespie to do the effects for T*he Long, Long Trailer.*

483 West Via Sol
# CHARLES WALTERS

Director, choreographer & dance instructor of Fred Astaire and Ginger Rogers & Gene Kelly and Judy Garland & more, built this 4 bedroom, 3 bath home, dubbed "Casa Contenta" in 1956. It has 2,518sf and a pool on a 15,682sf lot. In 1945, he was the dance

director for the movie *Abbot and Costello in Hollywood*, which included Lucille Ball as herself in an uncredited role and, in 1976, he directed the TV movie *What now, Catherine Curtis?* starring Lucy. Walters also owned Chuck Walters Presents, a resort wear for gentlemen boutique located downtown Palm Springs at 137 North Palm Canyon Drive.

## 372 South Monte Vista Drive
# WILLIAM BENDIX

Played the supporting actor role in the noir thriller *The Dark Corner* (1946) which included Lucille Ball in the lead role. Bendix resided here with his wife Theresa. The 3 bedroom, 3 bath home was built in 1948 with 1,606sf and a pool on a 8,712sf lot. In 1963, he moved to 372 South Monte

Vista Drive and then died a year later in December 1964.

## 504 South Indian Trail
# LESLIE CHARTERIS

Mystery author who, in 1939, wrote The Saint in Palm Springs while staying here. The stucco and tile 2,660sf home was designed by architect Walter Neff and built in 1935. It has 4 bedrooms and 3 bathrooms atop a massive 21,780sf lot. He also wrote the movie *Two Smart People.*

Ball played the lead actress role of Ricki Woodner, the girl-friend who in the end winds up with all the money of a stock broker con man. Her swindler lover narrowly cheats death, yet is still sent up the river to Sing Sing, leaving Lucy waiting.

## 1049 East Via Altamira
# VAN JOHNSON

Actor and his wife, *Eve Abbot,* bought this home in 1955. The couple lived here with custody of best friend, Keenan Wynn's, two sons (Ned and Tracy), who was a frequent visitor. It's often been speculated this atypical threesome was hiding a homosexual lifestyle for Johnson.

Van was in two Lucy movies. In 1946, he was the lead actor in *Easy to Wed*, which cast Ball in a supporting role opposite Keenan Wynn and, in 1968, Johnson played the supporting role in *Yours, Mine and Ours* while Lucille Ball played the lead.

## 1295 North Via Monte Vista
# PETER LAWFORD

The 5th member of Sinatra's Rat Pack lived here in the Las Palmas neighborhood during the Kennedy years. The home was built by George Alexander in 1957. It has 3 bedrooms and 4 baths, 3,410sf and sits on a 13,939sf lot with a pool. Lawford had an uncredited actor's part in *Ziegfeld Follies* (1946) which starred Lucy.

## 1380 Malaga Circle
# HELEN ROSE

Costume Designer for MGM lived here in 1978. It's a large 3 bed, 3 bath, 2,593sf condo, built in 1971, on a 3,920sf lot. She was the Costume Designer for the revue movie *Ziegfeld Follies* (1946) which cast Lucille Ball in a singing & dancing role and she was hired by Desilu as Costume Designer for *The Long, Long Trailer* (1953).

## 1128 East San Lorenzo Road
# WILLIAM A. SEITER

Director of Laurel and Hardy, Astaire and Rogers, and the Marx Brothers owned this 3 bedroom, 3 bath,1949 home in 1951. It has 2,119sf of living space atop a 10,890sf lot. In 1946, he directed Lucille Ball in her role as a faithful wife who takes gentle revenge on her philandering husband in the dark film *Lover Come Back.*

## 1580 East Mesquite Avenue
# CHARLES WINNINGER

Actor retired here prior to his death in 1969. His widow Gertrude Walker lived here writing mystery novels till her death in 1995. The 4 bedroom, 3 bath, 2,569sf home was built in 1948 on a 10,454sf lot with a pool. He played a supporting role in *Lover Come Back* (1946) with Lucy

and, in October 1954, he played Fred Mertze's old Vaudeville partner on *I Love Lucy*, season 4 episode 2.

## 1323 South Driftwood Drive
# WILLIAM HOLDEN

Actor lived here from 1967 to 1977. The home is large by Palm Springs standards: 4,409sf, with 3 bedrooms, 4 baths and 4 lots combined into one gigantic property for a total of 42,253sf of land. In 1949, he co-starred in *Miss Grant Takes Richmond*, in which Lucille Ball played Miss

Grant and, in February, 1955, Holden guest starred on *I Love Lucy*, season 4, episode 17, whereby Lucy was annoying him as he tried to eat lunch at the Brown Derby.

## 2466 Southridge Drive
# WILLIAM HOLDEN

Actor bought the land for this mountaintop estate in 1972. He first hired E. Stewart Williams to design the home but thought it too pricey and then hired Hugh Kaptur for a more streamlined house, which he built in 1977. The home is 6,657sf with 3 bedrooms and 4 baths on a 161,608sf lot with a pool.

## 1014 East Buena Vista Drive
# BOB HOPE

Actor purchased this home in 1941 and lived here till 1946. The 3 bedroom, 3 bath home was built in 1936 with 2,126sf on a 10,019sf lot. It remained part of the Dolores Hope Trust till it sold in 2013. Hope helped instruct Lucy and Desi in becom-

*1014 East Buena Vista*

ing production bosses by hiring Desi to be his Music Director for the *Bob Hope Radio Show* in 1944. This was Desi's first introduction into executive production meetings. Hope's second home in the desert was at 1188 East El

*1188 East El Alameda*

2466 Southridge
# BOB HOPE
Alameda. It was built in 1935 with 5 bedrooms and 5 baths in a 2,943sf floor plan located on a 16,117sf lot with a pool. Bob and Lucy did several projects over the years with Lucy as his co-star, including: *Sorrowful Jones* (1949), *Fancy Pants* (1950), Hope guest starred on *I Love Lucy,* season 6 episode 1, (October 1956) as himself, who Lucy spots Bob at a Yankee game and then tries desperately to ask him to perform with Ricky. In 1960, Hope and Ball returned to the big screen with *The Facts of Life* and they made *Critics Choice* (1963). He appeared on *The Lucy Show* (1962-1968). Lucy's last appearance on screen was alongside Bob Hope when, in March 1989, they were honored by the Academy Awards as *The Living Legends*. Bob owned two more Palm Springs homes. One was at 2970 East Via Vaquero Road. But, it is the home at 2466 Southridge Drive that is his most famous house. "The House of Hope" was

*2466 Southridge Drive*

completed in 1979 after it burnt to the steel girder frame in 1973. Designed by architect John Lautner, Hope owned this home till his death in 2003. It is a massive 17,531sf with 6 bedrooms and 12 baths on a 138,085sf lot.

2617 South Camino Real
# SIDNEY LANFIELD

Director of Bob Hope's and Lucille Ball's movie, *Sorrowful Jones* (1949), lived here with his actress-wife, Shirley Mason, until he died in 1972. The 3 bedroom, 3 bath home was built in 1964 and has 2,431sf on a 8,276sf lot.

## 2153 North Cerritos Road
# SID TOMACK

Supporting actor who played waiters, con artists and other assorted bad guys, lived in this 3 bedroom, 2 bath, 1,964sf home, built in 1960, on an 11,761sf lot. Sid played an uncredited waiter in *Sorrowful Jones* (1949) with Lucy and also played Bangs in *The Fuller Brush Girl* (1950) with Lucy.

## 1255 Camino Mirasol North
# BUDDY ADLER

20th Century Fox Head of Production and a founding member of the Screen Actors Guild lived here with his actress wife, Anita Louise, until Adler's death in 1960. Both were very big in desert charities. In 1950, he used his position to produce *A Woman of Distinction* which included Lucy in a cameo role.

## 355 East Valmonte Sur
# JACK BENNY

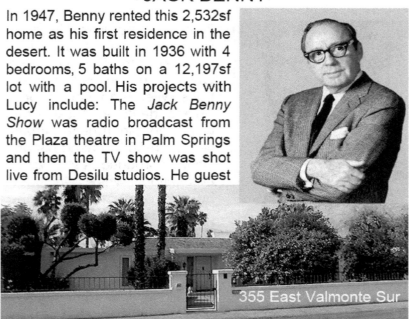

In 1947, Benny rented this 2,532sf home as his first residence in the desert. It was built in 1936 with 4 bedrooms, 5 baths on a 12,197sf lot with a pool. His projects with Lucy include: The *Jack Benny Show* was radio broadcast from the Plaza theatre in Palm Springs and then the TV show was shot live from Desilu studios. He guest

355 East Valmonte Sur

starred on *The Lucy Show* (1962-1968) and he was both the Technical Advisor and played Ollie "Sweet Lips" on the movie *A Guide for the Married Man* (1967). Benny and his actress/wife, Mary Livingston, bought this Las Palmas neighborhood 7 bedroom, 6 bath, 4,946sf home below in 1965.

424 West Vista Chino

## 2126 George Drive
# BILLY DANIELS, Sr.

Big Band singer who broke the race barrier in the 1930's lived here from 1960-1965. The 2 bedroom, 2 bath home was built in 1959 with 1,225sf of interior space on a 10,454sf lot with a pool. Daniels was a mix of Portuguese, Choctaw Indian, African American and was a distant relative of Daniel Boone.

Billy was the choreographer for the movie *Fancy Pants* (1950) which co-starred Lucille Ball and starred Bob Hope.

## 1066 East Via Altamira
# GREGORY GAYE

Gaye played the supporting role of Caliph Ali in *The Magic Carpet* (1950) which starred Lucille Ball. In 1975, this actor, known more for portraying German Generals and Russian royalty, owned this 3 bedroom, 4 bath, 3,127sf home, built in 1947 on a 17,860sf lot.

## 1385 East El Alameda
# FRANCIS LEDERER

Lederer played professor Paul Simons in *A Woman of Distinction* (1950) which cast Lucille Ball in a cameo role as herself. The Fifty year actor of silent films, Broadway and TV's Mission: Impossible owned this 3 bedroom, 2 bath home for nearly thirty years till his death in 2000. After which it remained in the Marion Le-

derer Trust until it was sold in June of 2011. The home has 1,981sf on a 12,632sf lot and was built in 1953.

## 448 East Cottonwood Road
# JOHN AGAR

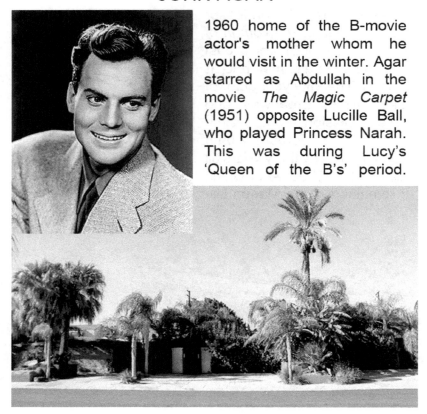

1960 home of the B-movie actor's mother whom he would visit in the winter. Agar starred as Abdullah in the movie *The Magic Carpet* (1951) opposite Lucille Ball, who played Princess Narah. This was during Lucy's 'Queen of the B's' period.

## 1280 South Calle Rolph
## MARJORIE MAIN

Vaudeville, Broadway, and film actress, Marjorie Main played Ma Kettle in the Ma and Pa Kettle movies. The 1948 home has 3 bedrooms and 3 baths in 1,869sf of living space atop a 10,454sf lot. In 1953, Lucy and Desi hired Main to play the supporting role of Mrs. Hittaway in *The Long, Long Trailer*.

893 West Camino Sur
# GEORGE NADER

Actor & Sci-Fi author and boyfriend of Rock Hudson lived in this 3,608sf, 3 bedroom, 4 bath home from 1991 till his death in 2002. It was built in 1961 on a 17,424sf lot and, in 2012, the home went through a significant remodel. In April 1955, Rock Hudson guest starred on season 4, episode 26 of the I *Love Lucy* show where he told a sad story about a man who irritatingly whistled so much his wife left him.

165 Santa Clara Way
## ALEXANDER HALL

Director of *Little Miss Marker* and other films owned this 5 bedroom, 4 bath, 3,326sf home in 1952. It sits on an 11,761sf lot with a pool. In 1956, Hall Directed *Forever, Darling*, which starred Lucille Ball and Desi Arnaz as a couple whose marriage is starting to fall apart. Hall has one other Lucille Ball distinction. He is the most likely candidate to have first introduced her to Palm Springs when the two would sometimes date during her, and his, early days of Hollywood in the 1930's.

## 377 West Baristo Road
# NANCY KULP

*Beverly Hillbillies* secretary and suspected lesbian died here of cancer while recuperating with her friend Joseph Baier in 1989. The 3 bedroom, 4 bath 2,464sf home was built in 1976 on a 9,583sf lot. Kulp played a maid twice in Lucy's projects. First, she played a hotel chambermaid in season 5, episode 15 of an *I Love Lucy* episode where Lucy tries to

find Queen Elizabeth II while in London and secondly, in the movie *Forever, Darling*, also in 1956.

## 38365 Maracaibo Circle West
# JERRY THORPE

TV Director of *Hawaii Five-O, Kung Fu*, and more built this 3 bedroom, 3 bath home in 1988. It has 3,085sf and a pool on a 23,522sf lot. In 1956, Thorpe was the Associate Producer for *Forever, Darling*. He directed episodes of *December Bride* (1954-1959) for Desilu Studios and he was the Execu-

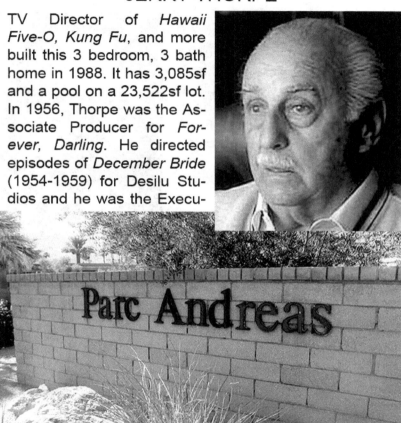

tive Producer for *The Untouchables* (1959-1963), also filmed by Desilu Studios.

## 666 Alexander Way
# HY AVERBACK

Actor-Director-Producer owned this 3 bedroom, 2 bath home in 1968. It was built in 1959 and has 1,225sf on a 11,326sf lot with a pool. From 1957-1960 Averback directed 101 episodes of *The Real McCoys* for Desilu Studios.

## 1070 South Calle Marcus
# KENNETH TOBEY

In 1951, the actor of Science Fiction films and portrayer of Admiral Halsey in *MacArthur* lived in this 3 bedroom, 3 bath, 2,200sf home when it was new. Tobey was also the star of *Whirlybirds* (1957-1960), as Chuck Martin, owner of a helicopter chartering company; a Desilu Production.

## 475 South Via Las Palmas
# RUDY VALLEE

Crooner & Actor owned this home from 1946-1957 when the address was 484 West Vereda Del Sur. The structure was later torn down for new construction. Vallee was in season 1, episode 1 (November 1957), where he played himself on a trip to Havana in the *Lucy-Desi Comedy Hour*.

## 1897 East Alejo Road
# FERNANDO LAMAS

Actor and his wife, Dahl, stayed in the 3 bedroom, 2 bath home of local Realtor Ernest Dunlevie as a guest in 1956. The 1,868sf home was built in 1956 and sits on a 10,019sf lot. In April 1958, Lamas Guest starred on season 1, episode 5 of the *Lucy-Desi Comedy Hour* when Lucy and Ethel visited Sun Valley, Idaho.

## 760 South Calle Santa Cruz
# EADIE ADAMS

Big band singer lived here. The home was built in 1958 and has 3 bedrooms, 2 baths with 1,317sf and a 7,405sf lot. In April 1960, Eadie and her husband Ernie Kovacs guest starred on the final episode of the *Lucy-Desi Comedy Hour*, season 3, episode 3. In 1962 she founded Eadie Admas Realty.

## 2290 Yosemite Drive
# WILLIAM DEMAREST

Actor best known for playing Uncle Charley in *My Three Sons*, a Desilu Production (1960-1965), first worked with Lucy in 1949 on the set of *Sorrowful Jones* as a supporting actor. He lived in this 3 bedroom, 3 bath home with his wife, Lucille Thayer, till his death in 1983. She continued owning it till 1997. It has 2,848sf on a 13,504sf lot.

238 Avenida Ortega
# MAX FACTOR, JR.

The son of the famous cos-
metics company founder, Jr.,
was actually born with the
name Frank Factor but family
urged him to change it to Max
Jr. He worked with Lucille
Ball and Bob Hope on their
first movie together after
Lucy's divorce *The Facts of
Life* (1960) doing, of course,
Fashion Makeup design.

He died in 1996. Home is now owned by Max's son
Andrew Factor. The address was changed from 297
Avenida Olancha to 238 Avenida Ortega in 1974.

## 1172 East Casa Verde Way
# MARTIN RAGAWAY

Scriptwriter for *Abbott & Costello*, *Ma & Pa Kettle*, *Partridge Family*, Brady Bunch, *The Dick Van Dyke Show* (1961-1966), a Desilu Production and more, lived here till 1989. In retirement he wrote humorous golf books. The home was built in 1974, has 2 bedrooms and 2 baths with 1,221sf.

Parc Andreas - South Palm Sprngs
# LUCIE ARNAZ

The daughter of Lucille Ball and Deis Arnaz, along with her husband, Laurence Luckinbill, owned two homes in Andreas Hills neighborhood of Palm Springs. One has 3 bedrooms and 6 baths. The other has 3 bedrooms and 4 baths. Both sit on 16,000sf+ size lots and have pools. Lucie guest starred on two episodes of *The Lucy Show* (1962-1968), season 1, episode 3, where Lucie is a teen-

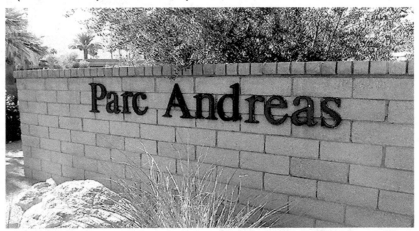

age friend of co-star Chris in *Lucy is a Soda Jerk* and another episode entitled *Lucy is a Chaperone.* Lucie Arnaz was 11 at the the time. She guested on a third episode in 1967 (age 16) where she played one of Lucy's friends in *Lucy and Robert Goulet.* She also had non-speaking walk-on parts in two episodes where she played a student or simply a person passing by. During the writing of this book, Arnaz and Luckinbill sold one of their Palm Springs homes.

## 71475 Kaye Ballard Drive
# KAYE BALLARD

Ballard bought Desi Arnaz's home in Thunderbird Country Club. It's a 3 bedroom, 2 bath, 1955 home with 2,094sf on a 9,583sf lot with a pool. Originally, the street was named Mashie Drive. It was renamed in Kaye's honor. She played the co-lead of Kay Buell, alongside Eve Arden, on *The Mother In-Laws* (1967-1969), a Desilu production. Kaye also guest starred on *Here's Lucy* (1971), where she played Donna in the episode *Lucy and Harry's Italian Bombshell*. Ballard still owns and lives in this home.

1877 Navajo Drive
# DON FEDDERSON

Producer of *My Three Sons* (1960-1972) and *Family Affair* (1966-1971), both Desilu Productions, lived here with his second wife, actress Yvonne Lime. The 3 bedroom, 4 bath, 2,430sf home was built in 1957 on a 10,019sf lot with a pool.

161 South Cahuilla Road
## POLLY BERGEN

Actress who starred in three Martin and Lewis comedies moved here in 1955 after divorcing the first of three husbands. She played the role of Clara Brown in *A Guide for the Married Man* (1967). Bergen also got the credit of Technical Advisor on the film. So did Lucille Ball, who played Mrs. Joe X in the film.

## 19 Cahuilla Hills Drive
# ZSA ZSA GABOR

Actress resided in this 1 bedroom, 2 bath home with a pool, which is next door to her mother Jolie's house, in 1960 between marriages to actor/singer George Sanders, hubby #3, and investor Herbert Hunter, #4. She was married a total of nine times. The home was built in 1958 and also has a gazebo with a view.

19 Cahuilla Hills Drive

Sometime after 1968 she moved over to the Little Tuscany area and lived there till 1988. During these years Zsa Zsa was married to three different men, one of whom dismantled her Rolls Royce in a fit of anger.

595 West Chino Canyon Drive

## 1123 South Via Monte Vista
# DEAN AND JEANNE MARTIN

Actor, singer, and suave #2 man of Sinatra's Rat Pack bought this 4 bedroom, 3 bath, 2,145sf, 1957 home in 1968 and then gave it to Jeanne in their divorce in 1973. Dino guest starred in an episode of *The Lucy Show* (1966) where Lucy was supposed to go on a blind date with a Dean Martin look-a-like. But when the look-a-like couldn't make it, the real

Dean Martin stood in. He also guest starred on *Here's Lucy* (1968-1974). Dean died in 1995. Jeanne still owns it as part of the Jeanne Martin Family Trust.

## 317 Camino Norte West
# DINAH SHORE

Actress Dinah Shore and her husband George Montgomery built this 1954 home with 4 bedrooms and 5 baths, 3,308sf and a pool on a 14,810sf lot. They built a dozen or so homes in the Palm Springs area together over their lives.

Dinah guest starred on *Here's Lucy* (1968-1970).

212

## 730 East Paseo El Mirador
# LAWRENCE WELK

Big band leader and variety television show producer owned this 2,749sf, 3 bedroom, 3 bath, 1952 home till 1978. It has a pool and a 16,117sf lot. Welk guest starred on *Here's Lucy* (1968-1974).

## 432 West Hermosa Place
# JERRY HERMAN

Songwriter, who wrote the music for Lucille Ball's play *Mame* (1974), owned this home in Trust till 2000. Home designed by Donald Wexler and Richard Harrison. Built in 1965, it has 5 bedrooms, 5 baths, 7,022sf, a pool and a pool house on a 58,370sf lot. He then moved to the South

432 West Hermosa Place

Via Las Palmas home from 1999-2004. It has 4 bedrooms, 5 baths 4,644sf, a pool and sits on a 16,988sf lot.

444 South Via Las Palmas

ERIC G. MEEKS

*Index*

*About the Author*

I'm a father of eight, wholeheartedly married to the beautiful and witty Tracey Wrubleski since 1999. Together we spearhead Team Wrubleski Meeks, specializing in Palm Springs area real estate. I'm also a lover of books and spend most mornings, before the sun rises and the kids are up, typing away at my laptop, preparing the next book. Sometimes, I just sit in my library and read or listen to 1980's mod/ska/rock on vinyl records or CD's. When I'm not otherwise pre-occupied, the family and I go the beach or to Canada to visit Tracey's family.

For more information regarding real estate, please contact me at Eric@PSCelebrityHomes.com.

I'm also an avid reader. Some of my most favorite recent reads include:

Fiction
A Storm of Swords by George R. R. Martin
Ghost Story and Side Jobs, both by Jim Butcher
Private Eyes by Johnathan Kellerman

Non-Fiction
The Pirates Lafitte by William C. Davis

Lately, I've been scouring book shops to compliment my next work. I just can't decide whether to write about Palm Springs True Crime, the story of Frank Sinatra in Palm Springs, the Masonic Civil War Conspiracy or, sometimes, I just think about writing a futuristic sci-fi saga about Space Pirates. We'll see.

Eric and Tracey Meeks